From These Hills

An American Family's Odyssey

By

Michael Moore

ISBN: 1-4033-9610-8 (e-book)
ISBN: 1-4033-9611-6 (Paperback)

This book is printed on acid free paper.

1stBooks - rev. 03/26/03

To Sue

*Very best Friend and toughest Critic
The Anchor of my Family*

Acknowledgements

If I have learned anything from this exercise, it is that writing family history consists of serendipity, surprises, and connections – particularly the latter. Not only did I meet new relatives, but also I learned that they *collected* things: letters, photos, and, most of all, *memories*. Maggie and Eddie West, Mary Lou Kelley, Imogene Baughman, and Forest and Lola Spriggs (new first cousins) gave of themselves generously and enthusiastically.

I am indebted to my daughter Amy who has been after me for years to get started on this project. With characteristic bluntness she asked: "What kind of historian are you, not knowing anything about your own family?" Then she laid on the guilt: "You are denying us the right to know where I and my sister and brothers came from. How *could* you, Father?" (She delivered those lines with an almost straight face.) She sat down, however, and read the entire draft straight through the night she received it and suggested several structural changes, which I have incorporated.

Then there are the libraries and librarians. Martha Kounse of the Hammer Collection at the Ironton Public Library, who knows Lawrence County, Ohio, as well as Maggie West knows Lawrence County, Kentucky, was so open and interested in our research. Similarly, Steve Charter of the Center for Archival Collections at the Bowling Green State University Libraries got caught up and started pulling items off the shelves for me to examine. He is the one who tried to connect "my" Perrys to the First Families of Ohio. The unnamed volunteers at the Church of Jesus Christ of Latter Day Saints' Family History Center in Perrysburg, Ohio, introduced me to their vast collection as well as how to use it. The staff and holdings at the Ohio Historical Society's library in Columbus made me feel good about being a taxpayer.

I owe much to Dr. Selma H. Calmes, chair of anesthesiology (and unofficial historian) at UCLA-Olive View in California who wept over my father's diary and then proceeded to share photos, documents, and stories. She became my West Coast research assistant and, more important, a very dear and gracious friend.

Finally, there are The Three Musketeers: Joyce Wallace, Gene Moore, and Sue Moore. They appear frequently in the narrative because they had major roles in shaping it. I felt close to Gene when we met in 2000 for the first time because he is the son of my father's brother – which is about as close to the Moores as I am going to be able to get after all these years. Joyce is an encyclopedia with an attitude. Her history of her side of the Moores is a work of passion, compassion, and humor of the kind that characterize elementary schoolteachers – the really good ones, that is. Both, moreover, have welcomed me into the family broadly and warmly, without question.

As for my wife: I think she got into this research in order to be able to visit with me now and then, and to make sure I had not fallen into the computer. But she got hooked and pursued census lists, city directories, and Soundexes like a bloodhound. She became a crackerjacker researcher and proofreader – and she was cheap. I thought that she would jump out of her skin one day at the Fort Wayne library when she finally tracked down my grandfather – sprinting out of the microfilm room to give me the biggest "thumbs-up" I had seen in years. (The librarians pretended not to notice.) Then, there was the time when she was trying to read gravestones in the midst of a driving rainstorm – but that story is in the narrative.

Thank you all.

Bowling Green, Ohio
2002

Foreword

This is the story of an American family and its determination for over 200 years to endure. Within that story is another, of my discovery of that family – particularly my parents – after paying little or no attention to them for most of my life. By finally undertaking that quest, I discovered the importance of kinship and love.

Throughout history, nearly all civilizations have depended on five social institutions to define and sustain them: (1) a legal-governmental system; (2) an economy for the exchange of goods and services; (3) religion; (4) an educational system; and (5) *the family.* Commentators, not only in the U.S. but elsewhere, have wrung their hands over the perceived demise of the family, and seemed to assume that an ideal model existed.

The truth is, there was never any single, ideal model – neither Ozzie and Harriet nor Archie Bunker. Families survived as best they could, yet celebrated their name and heritage. Mine certainly did from its beginnings in Virginia and the Carolinas, up to Ohio, out to California, and back again. They experienced hardship and sorrow, hope and merriment, and proved once again that blood is indeed thicker than water.

Therein lies its legacy, showing us how to understand ourselves better and perhaps live our lives more purposefully. That may not be a startling pronouncement, but in a society like ours, where reflection, serious self-assessment, and even history are not particularly venerated, it is an important one. In our push for individualism and freedom from nearly all restraint, we are learning that the line between liberty and loneliness can be exceedingly thin. Thus, a family – even a dysfunctional one – proclaims a connected-ness that gives dimension to one's identity.

My forbears were hillbillies and river rats – terms familiar in the Appalachians and along the Ohio River, where much of my history lies. Because of the impact of that environment, I must tell the story of places where they lived – Pound, Virginia, Flat Gap and Ashland, Kentucky, and Hanging Rock and Portsmouth, Ohio.

My family has never been rich or famous (though we came close a couple of times). It is ordinary. But in that ordinariness lies its universality – of people with strengths and weaknesses relying on one another to cope with events. There was alienation and resentment and bitterness to be sure, but there was also love and memory. Realizing at long last that these were *kinfolk* somehow gave it a special meaning.

That is what my odyssey did for me.

I

Iron and the River

It was the iron that brought my mother's forebears – the Slimps and the Perrys, the Smiths and the Yates – to Hanging Rock, Ohio, and its River.

I lie on the levee in the warm sun watching the Ohio – a living highway. Huge flotillas of barges, laden with coal and scrap iron, slowly make their way up and down the River, sounding their ear-splitting, deep horns as they approach the bridge. The bass notes ricochet off the Kentucky hills to Ohio's and back to Kentucky again – all the way up the valley. I call this place home and I summon my ancestors.

They came from Germany, Sweden, England, and Ireland, from Virginia, Kentucky, Pennsylvania, New Jersey, and Tennessee. They came to dig the ore *("Hell, it's lyin' on top of the ground, almost! All you'ns have to do is bend over and pick it up!")* They built stone furnaces that looked like miniature pyramids, made charcoal for the fire to smelt the charge, and poured the molten metal into vessels called "pigs".

At first, the men poured about a ton of iron a day. That's how nearby Iron-ton got its name[1]. The tonnage rapidly increased, however, as more and better furnaces were built. It was some of the best quality iron in the world, and if it were made with charcoal rather than coke it was even better because it was free of the sulfur that contaminated Ohio's coal. Thanks to the River, it could be easily shipped east or west to finishing mills and foundries that forged rails, bridges, girders, locomotives and cannons out of the pigs. Railroad construction extended the possibilities even further. Iron became the metaphor for the strength and power of a burgeoning young nation, and for over fifty years, the Hanging Rock Iron Region made more

---

[1] Unlike most cities, Ironton was deliberately planned and laid out in 1849 for the express purpose of shipping out the ore by rail and river and bringing in settlers and supplies. It provided lively competition to Portsmouth, 30 miles downriver, which was larger, older, and the terminus of the Ohio-Erie Canal.

1

pig iron than almost any other place in the Union. It helped win the Civil War and build the Transcontinental Railroad. It became armor plating for the *Monitor* whose battle with the *Virginia* changed forever the course of naval warfare. It became the barrels of Grant's huge siege guns at Vicksburg, enabling his victory there to split the Confederacy, an event nearly as important as Meade's defeat of Lee at Gettysburg.

These ironworkers and colliers – my great grandfathers and great-great grandfathers among them – worked hard at those furnaces, and the heat there had to remind them of the fires of hell. Their womenfolk held the families together and raised the children, taking them to the Presbyterian or Methodist churches located across the street from each another. They nursed their husbands, and somehow "made do" with the meager wages. The families lived in the company's houses and were paid in company scrip, which meant that they could buy their goods only at the company store and pay company prices. That made them angry, for they knew they were being cheated but they could not do much about it.

My mother's early ancestors stayed on in Hanging Rock and Ironton and died there. The ore eventually gave out and the hills could no longer yield trees for the charcoal. Other cities like Pittsburgh and Gary emerged to make steel, and so later generations of family moved away to other jobs – almost all blue-collar and hard labor. Many of them, however, stayed close to the River, even when it became a fearsome enemy during the floods.

Present-day Ironton, Ohio

Hanging Rock gradually shrank to a few houses, by-passed by the highway. The cemetery is growing, though, as kin are brought back home. The road leading to it is much better than the old railroad bed that one once had to travel to get there. Digging in the graveyard, however, is still hard; one needs a pick to get through the shale, heavy clay, and tangled roots that lie just beneath the grass. But this is where my mother, my father, and her ancestors lie, and others will join them – next to the iron and the river that flows below.

From the Sea

Certainly, Johan Frederick Slimp and his wife Mary Metz knew nothing about Hanging Rock when they boarded the good ship *Sally* in 1767 for the passage from Rotterdam to the American colonies.[2] Johan, who was an ironworker, left his widowed father George Simon Shlemp – one of my 128 great-great-great-great-great-great-grandfathers (or 6g grandfather) – back in Kandel, Germany, to try his luck in the New World. He and Mary got a head start on their family when she gave birth to Jacob at sea. If they had been aboard a warship instead of a merchant vessel, the crew might have assisted her in labor by firing off cannons, as they did for navy wives allowed to ship out with their husbands and who had difficulty in childbirth. (Hence the term "son of a gun".) But young Jacob did not need a salvo to enter the world. Other siblings soon joined him, starting with Virginia in 1775, named after her new home.

In November 1792, Jacob married Mary Dougherty[3] in Wythe County, located in the Blue Ridge mountains of southwestern Virginia. (Residents there used to brag that you could catch trout barehanded in the river simply by reaching under a rock – if you knew the right one.) Jacob and Mary had three children there before traveling down what is now Interstate 81. It was called the Great Wagon Road in those days and not much more than a dirt path in some places. But it was a direct route from Wythesville, the county seat, to nearby Tennessee, where men made iron. They moved to Carter County where they had two more sons, Michael (1793) and Joseph (1797).

---

[2] This information was graciously supplied by David Lea and Lowell Slimp.
[3] He may have married Sally Shoun earlier.

There must have been more Slimps than just Jacob and his family because the census records of Carter and Johnson counties show legions of them. Michael married Hannah Netherley (born in 1803) and Joseph married Sabra Wilson (1803-1884). The husbands were also skilled ironworkers and were relatively well off, but their comparative affluence did not prevent them from being attracted to Hanging Rock, which in the 1830's was beginning to make iron in a serious way. They headed to Ohio, living for a while in Perry Co., Kentucky, and finally moving to Kelly's Mill, near Hanging Rock.

One of Michael and Hannah's daughters, Elizabeth Slimp, was only 14 when she wedded a "furnace laborer" named Lindsey Perry. They had four children but after nine years she divorced him, left her family, and in September 1854, married John Moles of Powellsville,[4] a small village practically next door. Apparently not too heartbroken, and needing someone to look after the children, Lindsey almost immediately turned to Elizabeth's first cousin Cecelia (or Celia) and married her in 1855 when she was about 19 and he 32. This marriage lasted, however, and they were to become my 2g grandparents.

Little is known about Lindsey. His parents may have been Samuel Perry and Margaret Lindsey[5], who are listed among the First Families in Ohio. Margaret's father, John, was the second settler – about 1796 – to come to Scioto County. By 1870, Lindsey and Celia had six children, including Anna, my great-grandmother. Celia also had her divorced cousin's four children to look after.

One of Lindsey and Celia's children was Anna Perry who loved to write poetry, giving us a glimpse into her parents' lives and work:

> I love 'em. 'Course, I am one of 'em, and I can't get far away
> from the hogs and cattle where I saw the light of day on a
> homestead – where I picked berries and my sister tended the baby
>> while my mother boiled the beans,
>> and the others looked over the greens
>> and if I got my work all done and wasn't very bad,
>> they got me boots with copper toes and let me go with Dad.

---

[4] The Moles moved to Letts, Iowa, in 1865. In 1874, they moved to Jefferson Co., Nebraska, where John died in 1909 followed by Elizabeth in July 1925, aged 94. She had 11 children and outlived seven of them.
[5] So claimed by Lowell Slimp, a descendant of Lindsey and Elizabeth.

My dad, he was a Driver. He drove a string of steers.
I remember every one, although it's 40 yrs
since I trudged along by Daddy and he hollered gee and haw,
and those tired oxen drew a load across a stoky straw.
Tom and Jerry were the leaders.
Dick and Dan, then Red and Roan.
Chuck and Turk, they were the wheelers
husky stages with heavy bones.

Mom, she didn't go along; she always stayed behind.
She had the Baby and 20 calves to mind,
And is it any wonder when I see a Boy in Blue
a-driving the milking cows? I want to be there, too
Or see a farmer down a calf and hold him with a vim
I simply cannot take a laugh, but wish that I was him.

Lindsey had a fondness for the bottle, according to my grandmother, who recalled that "he might be as drunk as a lord when he sat down to dinner, but still could say grace as sober as a judge." Of

A Charcoal Furnace – "Vesuvius" (1833)

course, drinking was an integral part of life – unless you were a Methodist, which Lindsey apparently was not. Whiskey, however, was safer to drink than the water, and it was considered an act of hospitality to press a bottle of spirits on a visiting friend or kinsman. He died in 1896, aged 72, still working at the furnaces.

Iron ore had been discovered in Hanging Rock in 1829. Much of it lay in veins a foot thick just under a thin layer of earth. Nearby was plenty of limestone, wood, and coal, essential ingredients of pig. A group of Welsh immigrants who had the experience and technical expertise came downriver from Gallipolis to mine the ore and build some of the first furnaces. Twenty years later, twenty-two blast furnaces were producing 56,000 tons of iron annually. By 1850, Hanging Rock's production ranked second in the nation, with over 2,700 men working at the furnaces.

Joining Lindsey and Celia Perry were Benjamin and Ann Yates who lived in Scioto County, next door to Lawrence County and Hanging Rock.[6] Born around 1790, Ann moved to Hanging Rock from Pennsylvania with her parents Isaac and Hanna Delong, and married Benjamin in 1820. He died a few years later, leaving Ann with seven children. In 1846, her son Isaac married 18-year old Rebecca Jane Lundbach (or Lunbeck) whose forebears had come from Sweden via New Jersey and Virginia. One of Isaac and Rebecca Yates' sons was to marry one of Lindsey and Celia Perry's daughters.

Thus, the Yates, Delongs, and Lunbecks – along with the Slimps and the Perrys – came from all over the East and the South to unite and be among those 2,700 workers – furnace laborers, colliers, wood-cutters, teamsters, railroaders, riverboat men, and miners. These were my mother's ancestors whose sweat and labor helped Hanging Rock and Ironton toward national pre-eminence as a major industrial center.

When the Civil War broke out, the Union's demand for Hanging Rock's iron became insatiable. More furnaces were built and production increased. People kept raving over the quality of the iron: "Only two other places in the world make iron as good as ours!" they boasted. Even so, Isaac left Rebecca and their seven children to enlist in Co. E of the 18th Ohio Volunteer Infantry. He was 33 and heeded President Lincoln's call for volunteers for three months' service. (It

---

[6] The name "Yates" is apparently derived from "Gates". A family crest depicts their origins as "gate keepers.")

was supposed to be a short war.) Isaac was mustered out that August and returned to the furnaces where he probably did more for the war effort than in uniform.

Isaac's son (my great-grandfather), James Buchanan Yates, was born in 1857 and was named after the Democratic President of the day. He was to continue that tradition when he named one of his sons Grover Cleveland Yates, a clear signal where this family stood (and still stands) politically. In 1876, he married Anna Agnes Perry. He was 19 and she 20.

James was a collier; that is, he turned wood into charcoal that fueled the iron furnaces. It was not an easy job:

> Forty to fifty cords of wood were hauled on sleds to a convenient point in the woods called the coal pit or meiler. The hearth upon which the charcoal was burned was made by leveling off a circular area forty to fifty feet in diameter. This location had to be where water was available for use while drawing the charcoal and to prevent complete combustion of the wood by fire during the burning process.

> In preparation for burning, first, a center flue was built up by cross-laying sticks. This pile of cord wood formed a cone thirty five to forty feet in diameter at the base and ten to twelve feet high.. [Then] the entire pit was covered with leaves and dirt to exclude the air. Small air ducts were left at the base so [that] the burning could be controlled. Firing was accomplished by dropping fire down the flue, igniting the chips and wood at the bottom and in the center of the pit.

> During [the] burning and drawing [of] the charcoal, great care had to be exercised to avoid complete destruction of the wood by uncontrolled fire. This required twenty-four hour service of a man called the collier who stayed in a shanty nearby... These men were a hardy lot, enduring much from the heat and dust of the pits and from the adversities of the elements... [T]he entire operation consumed about three weeks[7].

---

[7] Frank Morrow, *A History of Industry in Jackson County, Ohio* (Wellston, Ohio, 1956), 41.

Typical of families who were poor and had to follow the furnaces to get work, James Yates moved his family from county to county. Once, the company sent him to the South to teach his craft to the fledgling industry down there.

In James' day, each of the 46 charcoal iron furnaces in the Hanging Rock region consumed up to 200 acres of trees in a single year, and during the 90-or so years that pig iron was made – from the 1830's to the 1920's – many hills were stripped bare. This may have been another reason James moved his family so often – wherever there were trees to be cut and processed. When coal was discovered in nearby Newcastle, coke began to supplant charcoal as fuel, even though it resulted in more impurities in the iron. In 1887, Hanging Rock produced over 98,000 tons of pig iron of which only 12,000 tons were charcoal-fired.[8] By this time, several railroads had been built to supplement the iron shipments by river and to bring in supplies, including wood, for the charcoal pits.[9]

James, unfortunately, was not one of the "hardy lot" of colliers. In October 1901, he died of Bright's disease at the age of 44. In the blunt tradition of the Appalachian foothills, the doctor described the prognosis to my grandmother Maude who was only 20: "With TB, you cough your life away; with your father's disease, you piss it away." James' death left Anna with a large family to look after.

It was Anna's oldest daughter Maude who came, half a century later, to raise me from infancy and tell me about the Slimps, Perrys, and Yates. She had seen her father making charcoal and she had seen him die. She had seen uncles and cousins working the furnaces. She lived in houses that belonged to the company and she became a champion of the working class. She gave me a ringside seat on the nineteenth century and enriched it with an historical commentary that was fascinating if not always objective. She never hesitated in passing judgments. In giving me her version of the family's history, she had her pantheon of heroes and villains, and to make sure I knew the difference, she kept her infamous Black List close by. In large part, she *was* my family's history until I grew older.

Although she never got past the sixth grade, my grandmother was

---

[8] *Ironton Register,* 5 Jan 1888.
[9] One of the railroads running into Ironton was the Cincinnati, Hamilton, and Dayton RR, dubbed the " Charge High and Damn Rough Ridin'."

Anna Perry Yates

one of the four or five most intelligent persons I have ever known. She had a memory like a computer, a wonderful sense of the absurd, a deep respect for history (which she passed on to me), and an intuitive feel for the rhythm of language. She dearly loved music but I can attest that she could not carry a tune in a bucket. She would go through three or four key changes in trying to sing "Go Tell Aunt Rhody." She also had a sense of economic and social justice that was honed razor sharp by the iron and charcoal companies' mistreatment of her father and the other men in her family. Her sense of justice, however, never extended to African Americans, but then the American labor movement in its early years was just as prejudiced.

Maude bore the brunt of the house and child-rearing chores, forming the earliest of many resentments she carried throughout her life. ("I was named after the maid," she once said, bitterly.) She learned racial prejudice at an early age from a washerwoman named "Aunt Chanee" . The details are murky, but the 1850 census did list a Benjamin Chanee, age 25, of Virginia who lived with Isaac and Rebecca Yates. He was a "laborer" who could not read or write. He was white, however, and according to Maude, Aunt Chanee had been a slave. It may have been that she simply took her master's surname, a common practice.

9

After Emancipation, Aunt Chanee worked odd jobs in Hanging Rock and drilled into my grandmother the belief that whites and blacks should stay strictly separated. As a result, Maude and I later had some knockdown, drag-out fights about segregation and racism. They would last for days; neither of us would back away. In 1965, my wife Sue and I visited her to show her our firstborn, and were watching a program about Martin Luther King. "Maudie," as usual, grew incensed. When Sue opined that King was a great leader, my grandmother indignantly asked her, "Well! Would you want your little daughter there to marry one?" True to her roots, Sue – who came from four generations of Methodist preachers – quietly answered, "Yes, if they loved each other." Maude was thunderstruck and with a great effort not to say anything else, clamped her jaws shut with enough force to bend iron, and turned back to the TV. A new name had just been added to the Black List.

As a good Democrat, she supported William Jennings Bryan during the 1896 presidential campaign. Her cousin, Bertha Yates (Aunt Bird) was a Republican and supported McKinley. Maude did not like Aunt Bird much – another name on the List – and so they sat on the front porch in Hanging Rock that summer, furiously sewing dresses. Aunt Bird used gold thread in honor of Sound Money; Maude used silver, in honor of Free Silver. It was war at needlepoint, although Maude laughingly said later on that she had no idea what Free Silver meant.

She recalled the time when, as a little girl, she accidentally stuck her hand in a pot full of paraffin wax that her mother was boiling over a wood fire in the front yard of their house. It was apple butter time and the paraffin was to seal the lids of the jars to preserve the contents. Maude's concerns, however, were over her burned and throbbing hand and she could think only of getting over to "Aunt _____" who would hold the hand in her own and recite some Bible verses over it to make the pain go away. "You see," Maude explained, "she was the seventh daughter of a seventh daughter and they were the only ones who had the gift of taking pain away. Nobody else could do it."[10]

---

[10] This tale has its counterpart elsewhere in the Appalachians. One version is that it was the seventh son of a seventh son who cured children of rash by blowing into their mouths. Cf. John Fox, Jr., *Trail of the Lonesome Pine* (New York: Grosset & Dunlap, 1908), 99.

"Maudie Gracie" loved to tell the story about her grandmother Yates (a "shoutin' Methodist") inviting the other grandmother Perry (a pious Quaker who always wore black and kept her head covered) to a revival, or "protracted meeting." Such gatherings were major social events in the nineteenth century and would last several days. They featured teams of preachers whose voices needed no amplification and who preached non-stop. When one gave out another stepped in. These were not quiet or sedate affairs. Getting right with the Lord was serious and noisy business because the sinners had to make sure that the Almighty heard them and believed that their repentance was sincere. Hence the "sawdust trail," the "penitents' bench" down front, and for the more exuberant spirits, the practice of "treeing the devil" in which one would assume the attributes of a coon hound baying in hot pursuit of its Satanic prey.

Well, Grandma Yates was into the spirit of things and whooping up a storm, but Grandma Perry, petite, prim, and proper, sat stone still, not moving a muscle. Naturally, she stood out in that crowd and the preacher, disturbed by it, walked down, put his hand on her head, and said, "Woman! Don't you love the Lord?"

She looked up at him and quietly said, "Doesn't any fool?" Maude's timing on that line was perfect as she burst into laughter, but then she had much practice telling that tale.

Ambiguity and nuance were alien concepts to my grandmother. Although she had a tremendous curiosity about the world – we would discuss politics and history by the hour – it was a universe with fixed referents, in her case the Presbyterian Church and Franklin D. Roosevelt. When I was seven, I would march behind the local Civil Air Patrol as we trained to protect Portsmouth from Nazi air attacks during World War II. (For an air patrol, those people spent a lot of time on the ground.) It was April 12, 1945, and as soon as I heard the dreadful news being hawked by the *Portsmouth Times* newsboys shouting "Extra! Extra!" I ran all the way home to tell her: FDR had just died. It was one of the very few times in my life that I ever saw that woman weep. They had been through a lot together. How I wished she had been with me years later when I visited the Roosevelt home in Hyde Park, New York, and claimed so many memories in her name.

Maudie had Five Rules for Successful Living that she reviewed rather often for me; they were her unique blend of the earnest and the absurd, but in retrospect they had a certain utility:

1. When you find yourself up a tree, take a good look at the countryside.
2. Read everything you sign, but don't sign everything you read.
3. Always know which way is North and who is in charge.
4. Be nice to everyone, but never – *ever* – let any SOB step on you.
5. When in doubt, vote Democrat.

Once, when I came home on vacation from college and she was asking me about my history courses, I mentioned that we had discussed some "crazy Socialist" doctor from California, Francis Townsend, who was trying to give money away to senior citizens, and …

"Hold it right there!" she commanded with That Look in her eye that could nail one to the wall at 20 paces. *Oh hell! What did I do now?*

She continued, spitting it out: "I'll have you know, young man, that I was president of the Townsend Club in this neighborhood in nine-teen-hun-dred-and-thir-ty-two when he was the only politician that offered anything like hope to help us poor people get through the Depression. Your Republican friends didn't offer a damn thing." "Yes ma'am," I meekly replied and we moved to safer ground. (*My* Republican friends? *She* was the one who sold out and voted for Eisenhower in 1952, a traitorous act for which I will forgive her only when Hell freezes over. Whatever happened to Rule No. 5? But I digress.)

During Hanging Rock's prime in the nineteenth century, the mine managers (such as James Bull who had emigrated from England) lived in the fine houses in town, while the Yates' lived under their thumb. Their wages were low, there were no pensions, and men like my great grandfather Perry worked into their seventies. Small wonder that the family's politics had an edge to it. Ore miners at several furnaces went out on strike demanding wages of $1.25 per ton and enforcement of a law requiring that they be paid every two weeks.[11]

---

[11] *Ironton Register,* 28 June 1888.

Socialism became popular, and this region, along with the mines in Colorado (later made famous by the Wobblies) were the two areas in the U.S. that developed their own, home-grown, brand of Socialism – without any help from the European socialists, thank you. Maude recalled that her brother Ross dodged the draft in 1917 because of his views; war with Germany was a "capitalist's war." She had gone to the train station to see him off with the troops, but when his name was called, another man stepped forward and took his place. She seldom told that story.

My grandmother had been a Methodist in Hanging Rock, but crossed the street to the Presbyterian kirk to marry a member of the choir. She and Philip Smith, a.k.a. Callahan, were wed on Valentine's Day in 1902 and they soon moved down river from Hanging Rock to Portsmouth.[12] Callahan had two brothers, John and Gray, and a twin sister Callie, who lived in Ironton. Callahan had several jobs during his life, one of which was a policeman in Portsmouth. According to Grandmother, this allowed him to bootleg liquor from Canada – my cousin Terry argues that it was from Kentucky – in the trunk of a police cruiser. Given the deteriorating state of their marriage at the time, I wonder at its accuracy. She had little good to say about him, but other family members had fonder memories. Some thought him a "quiet, jovial man," and Terry said of her grandfather:

> I think he spoiled me rotten. I remember he bought me my first formal. I believe I was a freshman and our sorority was having some sort of dance. He took me to Tudor's dress shop [an expensive store]. I really thought I was something.

> We used to go to Ironton quite often and I liked that. Aunt Callie baked bread and sweet rolls a lot and I remember their house seemed to always smell like a bakery.

But then she added:

> Maudie never liked it when she found out we had been there.

---

[12] His parents were Henry Smith and Susan Sherman Smith. Susan died in 1931, aged 71; Henry died in 1940.

13

When Callahan and my grandmother separated in 1935, he went to live with Callie. I visited there after my grandfather's funeral in 1949 – Terry and her mother Anne were broken-hearted, but Maude refused to attend – and saw two razorback hogs that he had kept in a gully behind the house. They were there "to keep the snakes down," I was told.

Callahan and Maude Smith, 1944

Callahan and Maude had five children – Ralph, Helen (my mother), Anna, Philip Henry ("Phil Hen"), and Susan who died during the Great Flu Epidemic of 1919 when she was only four days old.

By the time of World War I, the Hanging Rock iron boom was ending. The ore was played out; the vast Mesabi ranges in Minnesota were yielding high-quality ore that was easily "raised" and shipped over the Great Lakes to Andrew Carnegie's mills in Pittsburgh or Elbert Gary's works outside Chicago. A single blast furnace remained in Hanging Rock until 1923, but it soon became a relic and with its destruction four years later, only a few iron rails and heavy stones remained to mark the sites where my family once worked.

The slow death of the iron industry was probably the reason why most of Maude's siblings had moved from Hanging Rock to

Portsmouth, 30 miles downstream. The city was energetic, growing rapidly, and locked in fierce and none-too-friendly competition with Ironton for pre-eminence on the river. Portsmouth had been the southern terminus of the Ohio-Erie Canal, which began in Cleveland and wound its way down the length of the state, carrying grain, passengers, and cargo. Although the canal was soon supplanted by the railroads in the middle and late 19th century, Portsmouth's gently sloping riverbanks encouraged a lively trade for the packet boats going upstream to Ironton, Ashland, Wheeling, and Pittsburgh, or down toward Cincinnati and Louisville. Several railroads supplemented and gradually replaced the river traffic. Portsmouth had become home to a diverse array of foundries, steel mills, brick refactories, carriage makers, and shoe manufacturers.

Two blocks up from the river landing stood the elegant Washington Hotel, one of the classier inns on the river where my grandmother worked as housekeeper, a management position of which she was extremely proud. One could rent a room there for $3.50 per day. That price included a private bath plus all meals – your choice of steaks, oysters on the half shell, frog legs, roast beef, pork, chicken, roast duck, turkey plus salads and desserts.[13] The hotel was located on Second Street, in the heart of the commercial district called "Boneyfiddle". This was the oldest part of the city and its original downtown. The stores, shops, factories, and breweries all wanted to be as close to the river as possible, even though it meant risking the periodic floods.

Just as in Hanging Rock and Ironton, the River defined our lives. In 1884, the city built the first concrete floodwall in the U.S. establishing a tradition of building walls tall enough to keep out the previous flood but not the next one. Thus, the 1884 wall would have kept the water out in 1881, but not in 1913. So, the city built a higher one and raised the streets behind it as reinforcement. Unfortunately, that 62-foot wall was helpless against the 74-foot flood of 1937, requiring yet another wall, even if it had to be built in the midst of World War II.

---

[13] Reminiscences of Ruth Beatty, *A History of Scioto County* (Portsmouth, Ohio, 1986), 26.

It is night. Although we are supposed to be under an air raid blackout, huge work lights illuminate the Army Corps of Engineers as they work around the clock to build the new wall. Will they be finished before the next flood? The river is rising. I wonder how a 20-foot high wall of concrete that is only three feet thick at the top can hold out a river that will be a quarter-mile wide when it crests.

The water is now half-way up the wall and still rising. Our house is directly across the street. If that wall collapses, we'll be the first to go, just like the Johnstown Flood.

The wall made it easy to visualize what life must have been like in a medieval city whose gates were barred against lengthy sieges from invading armies. No army, however, could begin to match the fury and power of the River when she was rising, sometimes as much as a foot an hour and forcing the Scioto, which emptied into the Ohio, to back up and overflow her banks. During those times, the two rivers merged, isolating the city like a tiny peninsula in a yellow, swirling sea. Portsmouth's people fought back, building the floodgates, filling sandbags, and waiting for the water to recede. They would move back from the high ground they had occupied during the flood, scrub the viscous, smelly mud from their houses, and then rebuild. In so doing, they took their place alongside the river rats of other towns up and down the Ohio, stoically refusing to surrender: *Damned if a little water is going to drive me out of my home!* But this wall has held and has kept the city dry.

Behind the floodwall was Second Street, running down the middle of Boneyfiddle. It was more than just a thoroughfare to our family. Although Maude's siblings lived in other parts of town, they orbited around Second Street. It was a concept, a part of my growing up. Second Street was home, the 'hood', a gallery of memories. By the time I came of age, Boneyfiddle was known more for its poverty and declining businesses. It was also a "tough" part of town; one of my early toys was a brick. It was more desirable to live "on the hilltop" – another clearly defined part of town, and it came to pass that your social standing in Portsmouth was in direct proportion to the elevation of your house above sea level. The social stratification was reinforced by the system of neighborhood elementary schools; busing and consolidation were in the future. Consequently, my school did not stand particularly high among the others and this was to carry over into high school. But it was my school and my street.

Looking into the past: Mural of Chillicothe Street in Portsmouth, 1940's[14]

As renters one step ahead of the landlord, the family lived in so many houses up and down that street for over 60 years that when we gave our addresses, we mentioned only the house numbers. Even so, the street and its residents were a given, inseparable from our lives. When I was poring over old census lists, I found myself walking that street and its alleys once more, visualizing each house and its occupants as the names and addresses appeared on the tally sheets. Across the street from Massie School was Mollie Langwell's cafeteria (745 Second), where you could get the blue plate special for 75 cents. Four houses down at 733 was the redbrick Gault residence where father and son practiced medicine. My great-grandmother noted the day in her diary that old Dr. Gault was found dead in his chair and I still recall the younger Dr. Rossmore trying to dig a wart out of the

---

[14] This mural, one of over 50, was painted by Robert Dafford as part of his Portsmouth Floodwall Murals. The murals, 20 feet high, depict the city's history and cover nearly a half-mile of the floodwall.

palm of my hand with his fingernails. My grandmother worked for Mrs. Gault as a domestic for $1.00 a day, and later I was to run errands for her.

Across the alley from the Gaults at 731 was the elegant, white brick residence of John Dice, a German immigrant and retired carriage maker who kept the brass nameplate on his front door highly polished. Dr. Jackson's home was next door; his dental office was in his living room. I could just see the top of his drill above the white café curtains that stretched across the window. Dr. Rose had his office at 713 and across the street at 716 was Mrs. Minnie Bates' rooming house.

Don't you kids know about the old lady at 709? And why she has that scar running down the middle of her nose? Well, one of her ancestors had had his nose slit open during some massacre and that scar has been passed down through the family all these years. That's also why she's cross-eyed. So, behave yourselves and don't you go bothering her with your noise.

Next to our house at 708 was the cavernous Reed Building where I nearly lost my two front teeth in 1943 or '44. During World War II, the building was a distribution center for clothing for refugees. My best friend Jimmy Morgan and I were playing on top of a pile of clothing; he somehow looped a belt behind my teeth and gave a good yank. They were hanging by a few shreds of tissue until Maudie pushed them back in with her thumb and put an ice cube on them to stop the bleeding. Her orthodontia remains to this day. A happier memory is my U. S. Army Airforce plane which I drove furiously up and down the sidewalk, shooting down more German and Japanese aircraft than John Wayne ever thought of doing. The harder I pedaled, the faster the propeller spun; my imagination took care of the rest.

On the other side of 708 was 712 with Grandma Yates (Anna Perry Yates) who was well along in years and housebound upstairs by the 1940's. While I do not remember her very well, my older cousin Terry recalls having to cut Grandma's toenails which "were as hard as iron." Terry also remembers the dust-covered hard candy in the bedroom but she ate it anyway. Other cousins had clearer and more vivid recollections. Mary Ellen remembered "just loving her" and wanting to be around her. "When I was little," she recalled, "I would

Mike, 1943

climb into her big feather bed with her. She was so loving, gentle, and non-judgmental." Alyce Ann also had fond memories of frothy lemon meringue pies on Saturday, the aroma of freshly baked bread filling the kitchen, and "the warmth of her pillowy breasts as she rocked me and sang, 'Where, oh where, shall the wedding be ...'" Alyce could still quote one of her grandmother's poems learned some 70 years earlier:

> I sit by my window
> and watch the folks go by.
> There are some that walk,
> and some that ride,
> and there are some that fly.

Those lines recall Sam Walter Foss' "A House by the Side of the World" in style and content, and they exemplified Anna Yates' open view of the world and its people. She also had an eye for detail, as she described the 1937 Ohio River Flood from her upstairs window:

Jan. 22, 1937: I had to move today. Went down the street to 515. Water was in the alley back of 712.

[Jan. 25, 1937] This is Monday noon. Water is half up the stairs now and rising, and we are out of gas and electricity. Got a coal stove last night – good and warm today. Got plenty to eat. Ruth, Earl, Ralph & Alan & myself. Water was off a while but is turned on again. Pixley [Alyce's father] just sent over coffee from the plant. I killed one of my chickens today – dumplings and gravy, having beans today.

Anna wrote about the furniture, dead cats, and chickens floating down Second Street. Water got into the Portsmouth Candy Co. warehouse, and its contents joined the debris. She hated having to boil the river's water for drinking but was grateful that her daughters, Ruth, Kathryn, and Dorothy, and their families were safe "on the hilltop, good thing." Maude was safe, too, in Chillicothe with Anne and Terry.

Much of Grandma Yates' time was spent in cooking for the menfolk: "4 men like Earl, Alan, Ralph & Phil can get away with a lot of grub. The boys are playing cards; forgot to bring our Bingo game."

At the age of 84 she was no longer able to get out and about, but she still watched the world through her window:

Jan. 2, 1942 Good morning. Feeling better this morning; headache gone. Ate a good breakfast – toast & coffee and a slice of bacon.
Well now, let's see what we will have for lunch since no one is here,
but Alan and Ross and me
think we can make out on crackers and tea.
That's a rhyme
if you take it in time.
I didn't mean it to be
I just thought of crackers and tea.

And now, for diner tonight: potatoes … and sauer kraut. What do you say, boys?
So be it. Hope I don't have nightmares.
Good night.

Jan. 18, 1942 Good morning. A nice winter Sunday morning, but cold. Sun shining bright. Church bells ringing; I can tell Old Bigelow's bell from all the rest. I wonder how long it will be before

20

it rings for me. I feel fine this morning but not able to get downstairs.

Well, getting along toward noon. Someone is calling "When do we eat?"

We have leftovers for Sunday evening. So don't expect much if you drop in.

Good night.

When my grandmother's birthday came on January 16, Anna wrote of the event with a great deal of tenderness, recalling the birth of her 61-year-old daughter as "a precious gift – a beautiful girl baby". This is ironic, considering Maude's continued resentment at being named after the maid. No other incident in my memory so marked the difference between the two. In a later entry, Anna mentioned Maude's "little grandson who lived next door" and took note of a trait that was to distinguish me throughout the family – my ability to ask questions non-stop that gave grownups heartburn. All grownups, that is, except Grandma Yates:

> **Feb. 21, 1942** My little [great]grandson said to me, "Grandma, is today tomorrow?" So, what shall I tell him? Tomorrow – so time goes on and where does it go – into Eternity? I suppose we live through it and yet we don't realize it in the morning . Another day (and so on). Such is life.
> Good night.

Anna was as resilient as she was humorous and whimsical. When her son Harry died, she struggled with her grief over several days, but was soon able to give it perspective and resolution:

> **Mar. 10, 11, 22, 23, 1942** Don't say he died; just say he passed away. Poor Sarah did everything for him she could ... How I will miss him. He came to see me every day as long as he could ... Well, he is at rest now; that cough was terrible; it comes to all in time. We don't know who will be next; the family circle is broken....
>
> What are we going to do about this old war? Don't you think it will ever be over and what can we do about it? I just lost a son, but thank God he died at home in his bed ... no difference if he died at home or in the war zones; he died in the army of Jesus.

Anna's "precious baby" Maude was having similar struggles with the death of her oldest son and her fears for her youngest who was in the Army fighting in North Africa. She lacked, however, her mother's tranquility or her ability to cope and reflect. My grandmother never did find the kind of peace that came to my great-grandmother. But then, few did.

Grandma Yates' house at 712 seemed to be a family center; her children continuously moved in and out. Dorothy lived there until she married, followed by Kathryn who was there for a while with her husband Lewis Adams, a foreman at the steel mill. Maude's brother Ross, the Socialist draft-dodger (and genial drinker) was a permanent resident. He would sit on the steps of the Reed Building and tell me stories about his pink billy goats. I knew the goats were make-believe, but I'm not sure he did. I think my grandmother liked him, but disapproved of some of his habits, such as his drinking, or the way he got his supply of hats. It was the custom for the men at the final Cincinnati Reds baseball game to throw their boaters (straw hats) on to the field to mark the end of the season, but he gathered rather than tossed. Ross' wife Agnes was a humorless woman who would walk into our house announcing herself as "Company! Company!" for no apparent reason. She once won $100 at bingo and spread the ten-dollar bills out in her lap for us to stare at. That may have been a high point in her life.

Uncle Ross worked for the city department of streets and sewers, and died in one after trying vainly to save the life of his friend "Jitney" Williams, a black man[15]. (I wonder what my racist grandmother thought of that.) The irony is that in trying to rescue Jitney, Ross was overcome by sewer gas and his body blocked the pipe causing the water to back up and drown them both. Maude sent me out to Aunt Dorothy's house in nearby Friendship to tell her the news; all Aunt Dot could do was to moan his nickname: "Not Hickory! Not him!".

Greater love hath no man than this: That he lay down his life for his friends. The pink billy goats will miss you, Uncle Ross. So will I.

---

[15] *Portsmouth Times,* 19 Sep 1951.

While Ross, Agnes, Grandma, and assorted Yates' lived upstairs, other cousins, the Croppers, lived downstairs. Jack Cropper – whose ancestry extended back 13 generations to 16th century Lancashire, England – had played football for Portsmouth High School in the 1920's, which was about the same time as my father and uncles. He became a fire fighter, eventually advancing to assistant chief. His wife Ruth was a daughter of Maude's brother Allen, but we never got along with them. Jerry, their youngest son, and I fought often, throwing rotten paw-paws at each other across the backyard fence. He was four years older and had better aim. That may have been the reason Maude refused to speak to the Croppers for over 20 years. I was never quite sure; all I knew was that Aunt Ruth was on the Black List.

One day, however, when the Rev. Laurence Hucksoll of the First Presbyterian Church stopped by – preachers made house calls then – she unburdened her conscience about her silence to Ruth, also a member of the church. Rev. Hucksoll urged Maude to greet her charitably after services on Sunday and offer the hand of reconciliation.

> Maude (*apparently distressed*): But what if Ruth doesn't say anything?
> Rev. Hucksoll (*soothingly*): That's not your worry, Mrs. Smith. You will have done your Christian duty.
> Maude (*with wide-eyed innocence*): You mean, that's all I have to do?
> Rev. Hucksoll (*completely taken in*): Yes, my dear.

She grinned like a wolf. I knew what was coming. She could hardly wait until Sunday. We always sat in the back pew and could get to the narthex first as soon as the services ended. There Maude waited, ready to pounce. Poor Ruth never knew what hit her when she was greeted like a long-lost lamb. Sugar would not have melted in my grandmother's mouth. Ruth was so surprised that she snapped her jaws shut and stalked downstairs without a word, while Maude retired from the arena justified in the eyes of the Lord. (Well, at least she got a thumbs up from Rev. Hucksoll, and never felt bad about resuming her silence with the Croppers.)

Maude's other brother, Grover Cleveland Yates, seemed to be the one member of the family who had any money. Mary Ellen remembers him as a "real gentleman" whereas Alyce saw him as distant and formal. He would pronounce "helicopter" as "heel-icopter" so as not to appear as though he were swearing. He had worked many years as a freight conductor for the N & W Railroad until a disability forced early retirement. Unlike the rest of the family members who were constantly moving from house to house, he and Lucy Bishop (his first wife whose parents had emigrated from Germany) bought an apartment building on Fifth Street before 1920 and stayed there the rest of their lives. They had a son James, named after Grover's father, the charcoal collier. When Lucy died in 1933, Grover married Nell Praither of Wheelersburg, just up the river from Portsmouth and near Grandma Yates' birthplace at Junior Furnace.

One time, on the way to Hanging Rock, Uncle Grover began to recite some Yates family history, telling of four brothers who had come over from England to settle in Pennsylvania, New York, Virginia, and Ohio respectively. That's all I remember and I could kick myself for not following up on it with him. Subsequent correspondence with other Yates researchers, however, has revealed that the story of four (or five) brothers is widely told without much documentation, and that no one so far knows anything about the origins of our branch of this very large clan.

Thanks to the Internet, however, I met Grover's granddaughter-in-law who lives in Indiana and who was researching her husband's family tree. She had sent out an inquiry and I gladly filled her in with what I knew. It was gratifying to learn that Grover's son James named one of his two children James, who in turn gave to one of his sons the middle name of James. That name has now been kept alive in the family for five generations.

I knew Maude's sisters better than her brothers. Another aunt, Ruth – not Jack Cropper's wife – worked at the dry goods counter at Bragdon's department store on Chillicothe Street. In contrast to the fiery Maude, she was so gentle – downright sweet – that one wondered how they could be sisters. Maude joked that Ruth had to have been left on the doorstep by someone else when she was born; she was too much of a Christian to be a Yates.

Aunt Kate had the reputation of being the intellectual-cum-tomboy of the family. When a young girl, she had TB, and although nine months in Arizona had cured her, she was never in robust health. She married Lewis Adams II and they moved into 712 for a while. Descended from German stock on his mother's side, Uncle Lew worked at the steel mill, laughed easily, teased "Maudie Gracie", and liked to cool his coffee under the kitchen faucet. When their son Lewis III was born, it was Maude – herself a new mother with Philip – who wet-nursed him because of Kate's fragile health. The Adams', however, moved to Dayton when I was quite young.

I liked my aunt Dorothy the best. Petite and lively, she worked on the second floor in the lingerie department at Marting's, further up the street from Bragdon's. It was "the" store in Portsmouth and she seemed to belong there. She was caring and practical at the same time. Aunt Dot had a way of tilting her head back and looking at me through the bottom of her bifocals – penetrating, yet kind – that just made me feel good. Shortly before I left for college, she took me in hand and marched me into the Criterion to order a suit, tailor-made (almost). I chose charcoal black and it wore like iron through five years of hard use. She believed in quality.

Dorothy was the youngest – the "runt" as she was affectionately known – of Anna Yates' children. Like the others, she put in her time living at 712 before marrying William Pixley who was a salesman and vice-president of the Ohio Valley Coffee Company. About four o'clock in the afternoon, the wonderful smell of coffee beans roasting would fill the air up and down Second Street. Uncle Bill's DeSoto also smelled that way since he kept a supply in the trunk for his customers. His family had been in Scioto County for generations and were all buried in the same cemetery in Wheelersburg. They attended All Saints' Episcopal, which was just one block north of our church on Court Street.[16]

Dorothy and Bill had two children, Alyce Ann (named after each of her grandmothers) and Bill, Jr. I remember Billy only slightly, but Alyce stood out in my eight-year-old mind as strikingly beautiful, articulate, poised, and self-possessed. She had it all. I had an overwhelming crush on her; she was, after all, only 16 years older than I and thus the ideal Older Woman. Alas, she married someone

---

[16] Our congregation always had warm feelings for All Saints. In 1851, they donated $100 toward the construction of our sanctuary, which still stands. Anyone giving money to Presbyterians cannot be all bad.

else, moved to Dayton, and later to California. I was not to see her again for half a century.

After living in town several years, Aunt Dot and Uncle Bill built a house in the country near Portsmouth on a knoll they named Hickory Hill. Grandmother and I visited there often and one morning at breakfast, Uncle Bill asked me if I might be interested in going to law school – something they had evidently discussed before and probably were prepared to help finance. Thirty years later when college teaching – and its politics – became a hassle, I wondered why I didn't accept his offer.

Grandma Yates was not the only one who kept a diary. My mother's sister (named Anna, after her grandmother) wrote for several months in 1927, followed by a few entries in 1930 and '31. While not as profound or philosophical as Grandma Yates, "Anne" (who was, after all, only 17 at the time) chattered about high school, cute boys, parties, movies, dates, trips "back home" to Ironton, and girlfriends. Her occasional references to the family suggested a great deal of interaction between her generation and her mother's. She wrote about her sister Helen who had been in a car wreck with Bill Moore, a slightly built but scrappy football player; they were to become my parents. She mentioned her older brother Ralph, who was on the road as a drummer and singer in a band. Ralph was known around Portsmouth as "The Three-Fingered Dove" – a reference to his singing ability as well as the fact that a factory accident left only three digits on one hand.

In 1930, Anne took a job in Huntington, West Virginia, became pregnant with Terry, and in March 1931, returned to Portsmouth "to stay." By this time, the Depression had taken hold. Family members were being laid off and were moving in with each other to try to save money (although Callahan had moved away from Maude and lived with Anne at 950 Second Street). Despite the hard times, there still were gatherings and parties. Callahan took "Phil Hen" swimming; the Pixleys, Adams and Moores went to Cox's camp for the weekend; and Bill and Helen celebrated their second wedding anniversary and "had a big time last night." Anne also constantly wrote about going to the movies – two hours of escape from the world in a warm place for only ten or 25 cents. She sometimes went twice in a single day. It was a ritual that my grandmother maintained into the 1940's and '50's – this time with her "little grandson" in tow.

This was the family history that I had known most of my life. It was a series of experiences, feelings, and stories filtered largely through Maude's perspective. Most of the tale was missing, however, because I knew nothing of the Moores, and I also needed to develop my own perspective and meanings of the experiences I already had.

Bill Moore and Helen Smith, 1920's

II

Route 23

Discovery

The family history that I had known for the first sixty years of my life was all one-sided and handed to me on a platter. One rainy Sunday afternoon I pestered my grandmother about my lineage. She sat me down with paper and pencil and proceeded to dictate from memory some five generations of Yates, Slimps, and Perrys – in order of birth. She was amazingly accurate and subsequent checking of census and death records revealed few mistakes; it became the framework for the previous chapter. In that recital, however, she did not mention the Moores. But then, I didn't ask.

I knew that my parents had moved to California and that I had been born there. My father had died of tuberculosis six months later. My mother had returned to Portsmouth with me to live with my grandmother, but remarried, and moved back to California with my stepfather, Bryant Sangston. I remained with Maude, however, and was visited about four or five times between 1943 and 1950 by Helen and Bryant until they divorced in 1950. At that time we lost all contact with her; I just assumed that she had died. I knew that Bill Moore had brothers and sisters whose names all began with the letter B, but I did not even know how many there were. We never saw any of them, except once.

Not talking or even thinking about the Moores just seemed, as I was growing up, to be as natural as the *de facto* segregation that kept all of Portsmouth's African Americans in one part of town (euphemistically called the North End) and in one elementary school that just happened to be in its center. Even in high school, although they played major roles on our athletic teams, "they" ate in one part of the cafeteria and kept to themselves. Few questioned it or even thought it strange – or else they kept their silence.[17] So it was with my father's family. For me, they never existed. Consequently, a number of assumptions and beliefs created a history that I had come to accept as true.

All of that changed dramatically in 1999, when my wife, a hospice social worker, came home from work and told me about an extraordinary visit that she had made. Sue's patient was a computer nerd who wanted to show off his new software, the Social Security Death Index. He invited her to try it and on a whim she typed in the name of my mother, Helen Sangston. To her utter astonishment she read that her death was not in the 1950's as I had thought but in 1984, 30-plus years later! When she told me what she had learned, I was as stunned as she, for it blew a huge hole in the history that I had nurtured for so many years.

I wrote to Sacramento for her death certificate and learned that my mother had died of breast cancer in a Los Angeles nursing home. She had been cremated and her ashes scattered over the Pacific Ocean. More letters, e-mails and telephone calls to California followed – the nursing home, her physician, the courts, welfare agencies, the police, state hospitals, MediCal, the mortuary. Nobody, however, seemed to know anything. The only thing I learned from these early attempts was that all medical and social services records in California are destroyed seven years after they become inactive.

What had happened after her divorce? If I could locate Bryant, could he or his family tell me anything? Was there anyone to look after her? What kind of nursing home cared for her? Most important,

---

[17] When my wife's sister invited a black classmate at a high school mixer to dance with her, she was called into the Dean's office the following week and severely reprimanded. When her father, who by this time was a Methodist District Superintendent, heard of the incident, he called and reprimanded the Dean. Such was the status of race relations in Portsmouth in the 1950s.

why did she not try to contact us during all those years? Why didn't we?

Another surprise awaited us. Sue and I were on tour in Ireland and visited the great harbor at Cobh in County Cork from which millions of Irish had embarked for ports throughout the British Empire and beyond. One can view the train station (now an emigration museum) next to the docks where ships once received the travelers directly from the trains and then set sail. On the quay, there is a bronze statue of a young woman and her two brothers – the first people to be processed at Ellis Island when it opened in New York City in 1893. The girl's name: *Annie Moore*.

My God! Were they *kin*? I looked at the statue of this small, brave colleen setting out with her brothers for a new land and began to appreciate how tough these people had to be in order to survive, no matter how young. I turned to a fellow traveler who had become a good friend to Sue and me. Tears were streaming down her face because this was the place from which her great-grandmother had left for America. It was an emotional time for all of us.

Annie Moore and her brothers

It turned out that Annie was not a direct relative; she moved to Indiana and then to Texas where she died in 1923. But that statue came alive for me, and from that moment, I *knew* that my DNA was lying around Ireland somewhere (probably in a pub). And I had to know how the Moores got from Ireland to Portsmouth. It was then I realized how little I knew about my father or his family. I had put off too long doing anything about him or my mother.

So began a search that has produced two interlocking stories. One story consists of the relatives and their tales, stretching back at least to the American Revolution – of cousins and great-aunts from Ohio, Texas, Michigan, Kentucky, West Virginia, and Virginia whom I never knew existed until a short time ago. The other story is about the search process itself that filled in and corrected parts of my grandmother's narrative. There, Sue and I encountered an anesthesiologist from California who cared about my father though they had never met. We also met Mormon librarians, kindly genealogists who traveled through cyberspace with us, and fanatic little old ladies in reading rooms who cranked microfilm machines with the fervor of *samurai.* Old jokes about hillbillies versus flatlanders reappeared and half-remembered images assumed clearer form. Each new experience shaped and was shaped by the previous ones. As our son Andrew put it, he only knew half of himself before reading this history. The same was true for me as I wrote it.

According to Joyce Browning, former editor of the *MOORE NEWS*:

> The Moore surname came to America early, 1620 in Virginia and on the Mayflower in New England. The surname has had centuries to grow and multiply.
>
> Moore is a very difficult name to research because there are so many of them.
>
> … But particularly, because many Moore sons were early migrants to Piedmont Virginia and out of Virginia, migrating both north and south.
>
> The surname settled originally in the James/York peninsula where many colonial records are lost. These counties, referred to as "burned counties," lie between the James River and the

Rappahannock River and were the most populous counties in Virginia in the early 1700s. Can't tell you how many of these second century Moores had seven or eight sons - most of whom set the pattern of moving away from the home county seeking virgin land on which to settle and raise their families. Their numerous sons and daughters kept right on moving.

She went on to discuss the difficulties of tracking "the numerous sons and daughters" and prescribed a solution:

With a well indexed, full compilation of early Virginia Moores, researchers can quickly follow a given name, find that he or she doesn't match the profile needed, and eliminate those who won't work. I've been able to trace my own Moore line in this very manner. I warn you now that the index for John, William, and James Moore will each probably be more than one page long.

Boy, did they love those names! By 1810, after the Scotch-Irish migration into the Valley of Virginia, there are 46 Moores named James in Virginia, 39 named William, and 34 named John. And that's only in Virginia.

Who was it who said that genealogy is 75% elimination and 25% discovery? In Virginia this is a clear truth because of the loss of the first century of history (and more) in some Virginia counties.

The other clear truth is that unless we have [a] reasonable means of separating out the Virginia Moore surname, then we can't straighten out the Moore surname in America.

Thus warned, I sent in my subscription for any forthcoming Moore index. I soon learned that some might argue that *nothing* would ever straighten out the Moores – land grabbers, hillbillies, philanderers, deserters, and counterfeiters that they turned out to be. Even so, they are *my* land grabbers, hillbillies, philanderers, deserters, and counterfeiters. And I have become close to them because the search for them became intense and serious and funny and moving. This time, the history was not handed me on a platter.

Pound, Virginia, July 2000

When U.S. Route 23 crosses the Kentucky border into southwestern Virginia, it climbs Pine Mountain and cuts through Pound Gap. Even though engineers have lowered the grade and made the road straighter by removing a good portion of the mountain and rerouting a river, it is still easy to imagine it much as Christopher Gist did in 1753 when he first surveyed the pass and blazed a trail for westward settlers. (Daniel Boone was to emulate Gist's feat 20 years later through the Cumberland Gap, 100 miles to the southwest.) Even with the improvements, Route 23 still presents a challenge to motorists. The back roads that branch off the highway – unmarked, lacking shoulders or guardrails often – recall the trails that early settlers made because there were no alternate routes – and there often still aren't.

Pound Gap

This is the country of the Moores and also of John Fox, Jr. who lived in nearby Big Stone Gap. Although his book, *Trail of the Lonesome Pine,* is nearly a century old, it is still powerful in evoking the beauty, tragedy, and mystery of the mountains. He spends pages describing the trees, forests, streams, clouds, and mists, recognizing their power in shaping the lives and character of the people like my ancestors who lived there.

You see, mountains isolate people and the effect of isolation on human life is to crystallize it. Those people over the line have had no navigable rivers, no lakes, no wagon roads, except often the beds of streams. They have been cut off from all communication with the outside world. They ... are the closest link we have with the Old World... They live like the pioneers; the axe and the rifle are still their weapons and they still have the same fight with nature. [Their feuds are] a matter of clan-loyalty that goes back to Scotland. They argue this way: You are my friend or my kinsman, your quarrel is my quarrel, and whoever hits you hits me. If you are in trouble, I must not testify against you. If you are an officer, you must not arrest me; you must send me a kindly request to come into court. If I'm innocent and it's perfectly convenient – why, maybe I'll come.[18]

Fox also wrote of the conflict that the mountaineers had with the miners and industrialists who came into their valleys to dig coal and iron and introduce urban values and ways of thinking. It was a clash of two different ways of life and perception, and although better roads, modern schools, K-Mart, McDonalds, and Lowe's have softened the differences, the older memories and values are still close to the surface. Self-sufficiency is important since medical, police, or emergency help may be distant; hospitality and kindness toward strangers are still graciously extended; and an occasional shooting recalls the old ways of settling feuds. The relative isolation and distance from help are compelling arguments to keep a loaded .38 by your bedside at night.

The touch-stone of all relationships is the family. An old joke says that, in the South, if you walk into a room of 100 people, you will be related to at least half of them. If, however, you are a Moore on either side of the Virginia-Kentucky border, the odds go up. The graveyards there – whether overgrown or carefully tended – are the libraries of those families. Each tombstone is a book in those libraries, adding to the accumulating stories of death, sorrow, hope, children, illness, and poverty, as well as the determination of those families to keep going, to procreate, to make a living, and seek better lives for their progeny. Generations of Mullins and Childers, of Cooks and Franciscos, of Wallaces and Youngs and Cantrells, are buried all over the mountains as is the family they married into – the Moores.

---

[18]*Trail of the Lonesome Pine,* 97-98.

When and from where did the Moores emigrate? Most likely, it was from Scotland through Northern Ireland. The family surname is one of the most common in County Antrim, hard by the Giants Causeway and a scant 12 miles across an often stormy sea from the Scottish coast. If, indeed, these were my ancestors, then they probably were Scotch-Irish and Presbyterian – a hellish breed of rebellious, stubborn, fiercely independent, and dour folk, who were extremely suspicious of any kind of authority, be it King or Established Church. They weren't too fond of the Catholics either, particularly after James II laid siege to Londonderry in 1689. Above everything, they cherished their freedom and were ready to fight for it.

James Leyburn[19] tells us that the Scotch-Irish came to America during the 18th century in five great waves, roughly corresponding to the degree of suffering at the hands of their British landlords, who, with their Church of England lackeys, effectively stifled revolt for over 700 years. The Scotch-Irish wanted the freedom to be married and buried by their own ministers and to have those ceremonies legally recognized. They were tired of the "rack rents" that jacked up their taxes to astronomic heights and impoverished them. They suffered when the linen and lace mills shut down, throwing them out of work. But most of all, they wanted land of their own. Land was everything, it was income and security; it was status and respectability; it was a clear sign of a man's moral worth and of his favor in God's sight. It gave concrete form to the idea of freedom. There was much land in America, just over the horizon.

Sue and I are standing on the sheer Cliffs of Moher on Ireland's west coast, looking out to sea. The morning is foggy and cold, with the sun just starting to break through the clouds. The waters are relatively calm and the waves glisten when the sunlight finally reaches them. Our guide is saying, "Well, the next parish west is New York," and the two lands seem very close. It is confirmation of what I had felt to be true several days earlier at the great harbor of Cobh. I can almost feel my roots.

---

[19] *The Scotch-Irish – A Social History* (Univ. of North Carolina Press) 1961), 171-176.

35

The Cliffs of Moher

Most Scotch-Irish landed in the Philadelphia area. Although there had been Moores in New England since the Mayflower, the Puritans had become as hostile to them as had the Church of England. There were not many decent southern ports besides Wilmington, North Carolina, and Charleston, South Carolina. Immigrants also had to compete with slaves for the menial jobs. That left the Middle Colonies. Pennsylvania boasted good, gentle land as well as a tolerant Quaker government. But by the middle of the 18th century land prices were skyrocketing and the colony was filling up fast, thanks to German immigrants, whose sober, industrious, law-abiding, and docile ways were undoubtedly more attractive to colonial authorities than were the hard-drinking, and combative Scotch-Irish. Consequently, later immigrants took to the Great Wagon Road – the same road that the Slimps probably traveled – stretching for 700 miles from Philadelphia southwestward to the Potomac, then down the Shenandoah Valley of Virginia, through the western Carolinas, terminating in Savannah. Up and down its length, from northeast to southwest and back again, settlers made their way to the frontier, seeking cheap land. Whether my ancestors traveled down that Road from Pennsylvania or up from the Carolinas is still a matter of conjecture. The point is what they did when they arrived.

The governors of Virginia welcomed these people because they made good Indian fighters and protected the Shenandoah boundary. Accordingly, the authorities granted religious freedom and legalized Presbyterian ministers and marriages. They were also generous with land grants which enticed later settlers like my 3g grandfather Isaac Moore to head toward Pound Gap. The governors of North Carolina also welcomed the Scotch-Irish, but later turned churlish and authoritarian when the settlers – called Regulators – decried the governors' neglect of the frontier and the practice of taxation without representation. Their quarrel escalated into armed conflict and became a dress rehearsal for the Revolutionary War.

It was into this history that my first cousin Gene Moore and I were

Mary Polly Cantrell Moore's Grave

ushered by our fourth cousin[20] Joyce Wallace, when she invited us to Pound, Virginia, in July 2000. For the previous eight months, the three of us had been in constant communication by email as we shared our research. Joyce was clearly – and modestly – the team leader in this effort since she lived in the middle of Moore country and had a head start in the research. Gene and I had done some work on our small branch of the family, but Joyce had the Big Picture and showed Gene and me where we belonged on a very large and old family tree. As we talked, we were caught up in her passion for this project, and as she generously shared her knowledge and stories with us, we happily assumed the role of research assistants.

Gene had not known much more about the Moores than had I. His father Bruce seldom discussed the family history and seemed to have

---

[20] First cousins have a common grandparent; second cousins, a common great-grandparent, and so on.. Joyce and I had the same 3g grandparents, making us fourth cousins. (Joyce's children, therefore, are my fourth cousins once removed, but they are my children's fifth cousins.)

limited contact with other siblings. Indeed, he never mentioned his brother – my father – to Gene. After a 20-year hitch in the Navy, Gene became a junior high math teacher for another 20 years or so, and had recently retired from that career. Like me, he had begun asking questions about his past and like me, he was having his history re-arranged. When we finally met, we were struck by our physical similarities – short, stocky, and white-haired. We had many stories to share as we began to reconstruct a past that had been denied us and seek connections that had eluded us over the years.

We gathered at Pound eager to meet one another face to face and to help Joyce, who was hot on the trail of 3g grandfather Isaac. While she had obtained much information about him, we did not know where he was buried. Neither did we know anything about his ancestors. Which one of them had come to America and when? Joyce had located an elderly relative who might provide the information we sought. Alas, the relative was ill and unable to see us, but Joyce had other things to show us.

She led us up a nearly invisible road to a weed-choked hollow ("holler") in Pike County, Kentucky, near Elkhorn, and about a mile from the Virginia border. When we reached the top with the help of a weed whacker, we picked up large sticks and began to sweep and pound the ground – to scare away any copperheads. "If you smell cucumbers but don't see any," Joyce warned, "head the other way and watch where you put your feet." We cut our way to the middle of the field where she proudly showed us the grave of our 3g grandmother, Mary Polly Cantrell, Isaac's first wife, who was born about 1790 and died around 1835.

Mary Polly may have been Cherokee – whether full-blooded or partial depends on which family member you talk to. Another legend is that several of her descendants are characterized by dark complexions and a bump – a "Cherokee Knot" – at the base of their skulls[21]. Surrounding her grave was a sarcophagus of granite blocks,

---

[21] Isaac Moore had dealings with one Isaac Cantrell of South Carolina who did have a daughter born about 1790, but whose name was not listed. Was this Mary Polly? We don't know. I do, however, have a bump at the base of my skull. A Cherokee Knot? Hard to say, but it makes a good story. Isaac laid the granite blocks to prevent Mary Polly's kin from claiming her remains and taking them to her ancestral home in North Carolina. Angered by this, they burned Isaac's beehives. (Pikeville, KY, *Appalachian News Express*, 15 Nov 2002.)

quarried, carved and set by Isaac from the creek bed below. I had not seen anything like it before. He would have needed a mule team to get them up the hollow. There were other headstones apparently made by Isaac – strange apparitions outlined in the shape of heads and shoulders. Were they sentinels protecting the dead against evil spirits? It was my first encounter with this remarkable man.

I would not have met any of these kin, living or dead, had it not been for an earlier encounter with yet another tombstone, this one in a Lucasville graveyard ten miles north of Portsmouth – on Route 23. Research in the Portsmouth and Ironton libraries had turned up the gravesites of my father's sisters – Beulah and Bonnie, plus Bonnie's husband Orel Spriggs and an unnamed child who died at birth. My wife had recognized Beulah's name on the graves registry, and I spotted Bonnie and Orel's name, just above Beulah's. What was missing, however, was Bonnie's date of death, something that we had to have if we were to follow up. In the midst of a driving rain at dusk – "a dark and stormy night" – Sue and I searched the graveyard and finally found their graves. On Bonnie's stone was carved the date of her death, Nov. 28, 1993. She was 95. We now could search the Social Security Death Index and learn where she died – San Antonio, Texas. A request on a computer chat line got an answer from a researcher who looked up Bonnie's obituary for us. He said that she had lived not in San Antonio, but in nearby Fredericksburg. Another computer search of the telephone directory turned up only one Spriggs – Forest and his wife Lola. It was Bonnie's son – an honest-to-God first cousin and the break we had been seeking. He then led us to Gene and others. Never, in all my teaching and research, had I hit a jackpot like this one.

It was a strange yet exciting feeling, calling strangers to tell them that they had a first (or second, or fourth, or fifth) cousin living in Bowling Green, Ohio. There would be an initial hesitation on both ends of the phone line, but then a name, a remembrance, a common event would be mentioned. The stories would begin and the conversation would quicken as yet another link was forged.

Joyce, Gene, and I traveled further up the hollow to meet other cousins, Dallas and Phyllis Cook, who owned the land where the graveyard lay. It once had been Isaac's land. They knew Joyce and gave Gene and gave me a warm welcome. Dallas had not fully recovered from an auto accident three years earlier but had learned to carry his pain. He was an impressive man – not overwhelming, but rather the kind whose silence could be eloquent, a man who knew who he was and did not have to advertise the fact. When, however, I asked him if he had lived in these mountains all his life, his innate dignity did not preclude a dry response: "Not yet." It was a zinger that didn't hurt, for he delivered the line in gentle good humor, with just the hint of a smile at being one-up over the visiting flatlander.

Isaac Moore was born in 1790 in Virginia or North Carolina. His father – another Isaac, possibly – had been born in 1752, but we know nothing else to date. The younger Isaac moved to Kentucky around 1815 or 1820 with Mary Polly and acquired so much land in Pike County that, by 1830, he became one of its richest 25 men, worth $3,000, a hefty sum back then. He also bought land on the Wise County, Virginia, side of the border; Joyce showed us the road that marked one of his boundaries. A Pike County court order, signed in 1832, appointed Isaac as a road supervisor and surveyor, giving him not only a difficult job, but also the information and access to still more land.

The land is definitely not the kind of tabletop terrain that characterizes my home county in northwestern Ohio; it is mountainous and fit mostly for logging. Isaac and his sons would cut trees and build splash dams[22] up and down the Tug River so that they could float the logs to Ashland, sell them, and head back down the road that a century later would become Route 23.

After seeing Mary Polly's grave and meeting the Cooks, Joyce took us to several county courthouses, showing us wills, deeds, and court orders pertaining to the Moores. As I stood in the Pike County Courthouse and handled the original court order appointing Isaac as road supervisor, I was reminded of Joyce's fond reference to him as "land-grabbin' Isaac". Equally acquisitive was his son Aaron, who was born around 1815, possibly in Scott County, Virginia. Aaron's future wife Lydia Elswick (daughter of Bradley Elswick and Catherine "Kate" Ratliff) was born around 1820 and was from either Virginia or Kentucky – the records disagree. In April 1840, he posted

---

[22] A "splash dam" temporarily held the stream back and made it deep enough to float the logs. When it was filled, a "keystone log" in the dam would be pulled out, causing it to collapse. The rush of water would carry the logs downstream to the next splash dam, and the process would be repeated.

a marriage bond of fifty pounds for the hand of Lydia and swore that he had no other wives.

I am dumbstruck when the county clerk casually hands me Aaron's original marriage bond to Xerox for my records – where are my latex gloves? I am holding my great-great grandfather, for God's sake! Had I longed for the Moores that much? I look at Joyce and she smiles; she understands.

Speaking of the Elswicks, Joyce discovered the following entry about the family in George Washington's *Journal of My Journey Over the Mountains* (1747-48):

> [N121751] Then surveyed for Mr. John Elswick a certain Tract of Waste and ungranted Land Situate in Augusta County on the Waters of Cacapehon and bounded as followeth ...

John Elswick, who hired Washington, was the father of John Elswick III, who was Lydia's grandfather. In other words, the Father of our Country once worked for my 5g grandfather.

Joyce Wallace has lived all her life (well, not yet) on the Kentucky-Virginia border and has taught school in Pound for over 25 years. Her experiences in the mountains have given her a wonderful sense of humor, a sweet and sensitive disposition, and the tenacity of a born historian. Her passion is to catalog every last descendant of Isaac Moore; she currently has over 24,000 names and 1,700 obituaries on file. When finished, her work will become the definitive family genealogy.

When Gene and I were with her that summer, she was trying to locate Isaac's grave. Time was running out, however, because there were so few of the old-timers left who could remember. A few months later, she emailed Gene and me to say that a newly found cousin, Ira Stanley, knew where Isaac was buried. Ira was over 80 years old, a World War II veteran, in good health at the time, yet surprised by the fact that the Commonwealth of Virginia still allowed him to drive a car, what with his bad eyesight and all. He had taken her to a remote graveyard that lay between Blowing Rock and Skeetrock, Virginia, literally in the middle of nowhere but close to the Kentucky border and only about four miles southeast of Mary Polly's grave (as the crow flies). There were several graves up there, mostly of Mullins'. "I enjoyed photographing the other graves, and was well composed at those sites," Joyce wrote. But at the next grave:

> When I realized that it really WAS Isaac though, I couldn't stop the
> tears. That old man means much more to me than all of the others...
> It really took a lot of me to kneel on the old man's grave and
> snap those photographs! I was emotionally supercharged and then
> I had to leave him.

Not "it," but "him."

Isaac may have been a big man – unusual for a Moore. When Ira laid his 5'10" frame on top of the grave with his feet touching the footstone, there was still a 16-to 18-inch gap between his head and Isaac's headstone. During the Civil War, at the age of 71 (or so), Isaac ambushed a squad of damnyankees who had shot one of his grandsons. When Isaac either ran out of ammunition or did not have time to reload, he tried to escape through Osborne Gap. That's when they got him, according to Ira. It was revenge and guerilla warfare in the tradition of the mountains.

Revenge is a recurrent theme. A cousin from West Virginia, Gary Mullins, wrote me about our common great-great-grandfather, Booker Mullins, who was shot in 1865 in Kentucky by a man named Hall. Booker's sons "took revenge" by shooting Hall and then fleeing to West Virginia to escape the law. Since three of Booker's in-laws were Moores, they may well have been among the fugitives[23].

Why was Booker killed? Was he the Booker, along with the infamous "Counterfeit Sol" Mullins, and James, Peter, and Spencer Mullins, who were indicted by a Russell County, Virginia, grand jury in September 1837 for counterfeiting hard money? Those boys were minting not only U.S. silver dollars, half-dollars, and quarters, but also Mexican and Spanish milled dollars as well. That would have been enough for a man to get shot, even 28 years later. There was, to

---

[23] *See* Henry P. Scalf, *Four Men of the Cumberlands* (Prestonburg, Kentucky, 1958) for an account of some of the more colorful outlaws and feudists of Pound Gap. The Mullins' appear prominently in the narrative.

be sure, a Civil War in between but mountaineers have long memories.[24]

There were so many Moores and Mullins who married one another, it is hard to sort them out. Joyce Wallace was not sure if this

Isaac Moore's headstone[25]

Booker Mullins belonged to us, but he was of the right age and place to have been. She added that the counterfeiting was so well done the government had to weigh the coins to see which ones were genuine. Sol had too much silver in his!

Joyce observed that "after Isaac [Sr.] died, the family seemed to fall apart. They scattered, some moving towards West Virginia while others returned to Virginia. Still others, suffering from tuberculosis, moved away to Arizona and other hot, dry states, trying to overcome that disease." It appears that "the family curse," had gotten an early start. Their houses were small and crowded, ideal breeding places.

---

[24] From the Russell County Order Book, 19 September 1837. Courtesy of Gary Mullins.

[25] Some family members believe Isaac died around 1865 because it would be more consistent with the degree and kind of military operations in the area.

Between the end of the Civil War and the Great Influenza epidemic of 1918, "dozens of them died of TB", or TB-induced diseases. In one case, it was the body of either Eura Moore or her sister-in-law Verna Phipps that was laid outside the house overnight after she died in the hopes of reducing exposure to the rest of the family. It did not work. Most of them died anyway, and legend has it that the house was haunted afterwards. So many kinfolk died of TB ("consumption") – Isaac Sr.'s wife and their son Levi Moore, Isaac Jr's son, John C. Breckenridge Moore, Cora Wright Moore and two of her three children – the list goes on, down to Beulah and Bill Moore (my aunt and father) in the 1930's. They were able to stay ahead of TB only by having many children.

One of Aaron's sons was John Wesley Moore, nick-named "Pike" after the Kentucky county in which he was born. He was my great-grandfather. Whether he was a Methodist like his namesake or not, he married a Primitive Baptist Church preacher's daughter, Martha "Patsy" Mullins (Sherwood's sister) around 1863. This was about a year before he enlisted in the Confederate Seventh Battalion and went away to uphold the honor of the South. He enjoyed a less-than-glorious military career, however, than his grandfather Isaac. As one account of Pike's outfit reveals:

> Prentice's men (7th Conf. Batt'n) have the reputation of stealing everything they get their hands on: & by association the others … have become somewhat corrupted.

That was a Southern, not a Northern, assessment. Lt. Col. Clarence Prentice was the commanding officer of the 7th. His second-in-command, Major Repass, was thrown out of the army for misconduct, and the other major, William Guerrant had this to say about his own unit:

> These new fellows … are about the greenest horns I ever met with… Prentice's men are [the] same. "I want some rations." "Where is yr requisition?" "Don't know."

> "How many rations do you want?" "Don't know. – Jist wants to draw."
> [This is] the dialogue between one of Prentice's boys & Major Thompson – the elegant Commissary.

44

Major Guerrant's brother, Edward, who was adjutant of the brigade, added:

> We are all very much pleased with our brigade with the exception of Prentice's (7[h]) Battalion, who are represented as a band of thieves & c. – Therefore, I made application to have them transferred to Gen. Wm. E. Jones. We don't want them.

John Wesley Moore, his Uncle Moses, and some other Moores were members of this elite band. John had previously served in the Virginia State Line but enlisted in the 7th on April 30, 1864, in Louisa, Kentucky – an ostensibly Yankee state. He was 20 years old, 5'5" tall, with dark hair, a dark complexion, and "yellow eyes." His enlistment record also said of him: "Young, ignorant, was deceived, served 3 months and then Dstd." The "Dstd" did not stand for "discharged." Great-grandpa went over the hill. It would be comforting to imagine that his French leave was occasioned by his disgust and moral outrage at the conduct of his unsavory messmates. More likely, he wanted to get back to his bride and the farm. There is some evidence, however, to suggest that he joined another unit – a common practice in those days. One can only hope so.

"Patsy" Mullins Moore was also a Kentuckian who was born a few farms over from John Wesley. When they married, they settled in Johnson County, Kentucky, and started their family of eight, including my grandfather Booker, named after his grandfather Mullins who had been shot by Hall five years earlier.

The different farms and counties on which Isaac, Aaron, John Wesley Moore and their progeny lived from the 1820's to the 1910's indicate a migration pattern that had started in Virginia and moved north. Joyce Wallace thinks that the Moores entered Kentucky at Ashcamp, an old logging trail that was nine miles north-northeast of Christopher Gist's trail through Pound Gap. They moved to Pike County, Kentucky, then up along the eastern border of the state through Johnson, Floyd, Lawrence, and Boyd Counties, ending in Greenup County, where John Wesley's son, my grandfather Booker Moore crossed the Ohio River into Scioto County, Ohio.

Thus, they followed what is today U.S. Route 23 to Pikeville, Paintsville, Louisa, Catlettsburg, and Fullerton, Kentucky, then to

Portsmouth, Lucasville, Wakefield, Columbus, and Bowling Green, Ohio (where I live). Other branches of the Moores migrated up the West Virginia side of the Tug and Big Sandy Rivers. It took the Moores 90 years to migrate approximately the same distance that the

John Wesley Moore at far left, about 1922. Two of his sons, Monroe and Aaron, are seated second and third respectively to his left

Slimps had done in less than ten – illustrating one major difference between farming and industrialization.

There is a formal looking picture of some of the Moore brothers taken around 1906 – as Gene Moore reckoned it, although I tend to think it was taken a decade earlier. It shows Grandfather Booker with his younger brother Aaron. The other men are Billy Cox, who was Aaron's brother-in-law, and J.D. (Jeff) Bond, who was Billy's son-in-law. Aaron, seated in front, is wearing a Masonic ribbon in his lapel. It is a formal occasion and they look a little stiff, spruced up in their good clothes, but Aaron's work shoes give them away.

Bonnie's son, Forest Spriggs, remembers our grandfather as a very kind and somewhat reserved man who "could do any kind of job – very skilled with his hands." He also drank heavily. Monroe was also reserved and much like Booker, whereas Paris (yet another brother) was jovial and outgoing. He also was a frugal man who, according to Forest, "did a lot of trading of goods and usually came out on top." Paris and Booker later worked in the oil fields that straddled the Kentucky-West Virginia border near the town of Blaine, where many Moores were born and raised. It is said that Monroe had

46

The Moore brothers, ca. 1890-1900
Booker is at top right; Aaron is seated in front of him
Billy Cox is seated next to Aaron; J.D. Bond stands next to Booker

to leave Kentucky for Ohio because he broke a man's jaw in a fight. He was not too reserved, it seems.

Neither was my grandfather. Several years before Booker married Stella (my grandmother), he "took up" with Emma Ethel Stapleton, who was born in 1867 or '69, the daughter of William Stapleton and Ester Salyer. Booker and Emma had three children, born in Elliot County. All of them married and raised families that grew to over 70 grandchildren and great-grandchildren. Emma later married and inherited a stepson. Small wonder that Gene Moore's mother remembered Booker as one of the black sheep of the family.

Flat Gap, Kentucky

Joyce, Gene, and I finally parted company after three days and nights of nonstop talking. Gene returned to his home in Virginia and I headed north up Route 23 toward Flat Gap, where other relatives were expecting me. I now was retracing as it were the steps of the Moores as they worked and farmed their way from Virginia and North Carolina. As I drove through the country, I recalled a story that Imogene Baughman had told me about a kinsman, poor Mort Moore, as she pointed to his picture in one of her albums:

> See, his arm's gone. He fell off a horse and it was such a break, and grass and dirt – no, not a horse – a mule. Someone slapped it on the rear and it bucked and threw him off. He was seven. So, they came to the house and amputated his arm. My mom said they did it on the table.

> The arm is buried in Lawrence County, in the old Moore cemetery. Then the rest of him when he was, uh, 18 or 17, he got killed – got shot and his body is over in the other county, close to the creek.

Although there appears to be little doubt that Mort (and his appendages) was (were) good and dead when he (they) was (were) buried, several family members had requested over the years that the lids to their coffins *not* be nailed shut.

> *"Not nail the lids shut? You're pullin' my leg," I say.*
> *"No sir-ee! Cross my heart and hope to die, Mike! Why, didn't you know that in the Middle Ages, people were so scared of bein' buried alive, that they'd have a cord tied 'round their wrists when they were put in their coffins, and that cord would go through a hole in the lid and the other end would be tied to a bell on top of the grave. Then, someone would sit all night by the grave – that's the graveyard shift – and listen. If that bell rang, they'd dig him up in a hurry. They'd say he was 'saved by the bell'."*
> *"Uh-huh. And if they didn't get to him in time, you're gonna tell me he was a 'dead ringer,' right?"*

I drove into Flat Gap past the Enterprize Baptist Church, where my grandfather's funeral had been preached. If any locale could lay claim to be the Jerusalem (or Mecca) of our family, it might be Flat Gap and the neighboring village of Blaine. I headed toward the home of Gail and Phyllis Moore Gillem; she was descended from John

Wesley's brother Aaron. Across the road lived Phyllis' daughter Leslee Pelphrey and her husband Paul Ray. When I knocked at the door, Phyllis answered it, looked me up and down, and said: "Well, you sure look like a Moore. Come on in; supper's almost ready," and she turned back to a stove that was heating enough food to have fed all the Moores from Isaac on down. Paul Ray and Leslee joined us as did Thomas, a grandson up from Lexington who had just graduated from high school and was going to study agribusiness. Leslee and I had been chatting on the Internet for several months and had traded information. She had brought a folder of information and family trees to share with me and I reciprocated with my notebooks.

Gail Gillem, who was Phyllis' second husband, had worked for the State Department of Education and then sat as a local judge before retiring in 1999. Quiet and friendly, he made me feel as welcome as did Phyllis and began to give me an update of recent Kentucky politics. He did not get as far as either of us would have wished because Phyllis called us to dinner and I sank my teeth once more into genuine cornbread. (A few days earlier, I thought I had died and gone to heaven when I sampled Joyce's sister's cornbread. Heaven had now reappeared.)

We talked as much as we ate, trying to fill in one another on the past 50 years or so of family history. After supper, they took me to the family gravesite in the high pasture; it required a four-wheel drive pickup to get us there. On the way up the hill, Leslee pointed out all the land that her great-great-grandfather Aaron had once owned – it was considerable.

At the gravesite, we again picked up big sticks and beat the ground to scare away the copperheads. We did not smell any cucumbers, but did have to wade through high weeds to find Grandfather Booker's grave. It is a small, simple granite footstone bearing his name and his years, 1872-1945 (it should have read 1870). His brother's tombstone was much taller and ornate, complete with the Mason's compass.

Getting this close to Booker had been no easy task. Several months earlier, Sue and I had spent a day at the regional Federal depository of census records in Ft. Wayne, Indiana. While tracking him down, we were confused by the existence of several Booker Moores in Kentucky. What we needed were his date and place of birth. We were able to narrow our search via the Soundex system to a few hundred possibilities that Sue proceeded to leaf through – one card at a time. She was about at her wits' end when the magic card turned up and she sprinted out of the records room as though shot out of a cannon. It was another breakthrough.

I thought of that afternoon in Ft. Wayne as I looked at my grandfather's grave and realized how easy it was to forget how hard life was for so many just a generation or two earlier and how that hardship often split families apart. Leslee underscored that fact when she described how Ashland Oil had acquired drilling rights throughout the region, intimidating the farmers to sell their mineral holdings for a dollar an acre. The company then proceeded to rape the environment and ruin people's health with the pollution. It essentially was the same story that Maude Smith had told me about the Yates and Perrys in the Hanging Rock iron mines and collieries. Times and circumstances are generally better for our generation, but we dare not forget what they endured. To do so would dishonor them.

We drove back down the mountain and to the family's pride and joy – their foxhounds. Each person had at least two or three and it was time to let them out for their evening run. Brown and white, graceful and fast, gentle and patient, there were two sets of animals – one set for competing at foxhound (not just dog) shows, and one set for running foxes. The show dogs did not run; it was bad for the shape of their paws. As for the running dogs, it was understood that they were not to catch the fox, just scare the hell out of him and work up a good sweat. As the family showed me their dogs and their trophies, I learned more about judging foxhounds in one evening than if I had lived to be 100. There could not have been a greater act of acceptance into their family.

Stuffed with cornbread and good wishes, I headed toward Portsmouth about 90 minutes – and a lifetime – away, where we had all lived at one time or another. Sue and I had done research there a few months earlier, but my discoveries about Isaac, Aaron, and Booker, and the late night sessions with Joyce and Gene led me back there to ask more questions about Bill and Helen, this time starting with his parents, Booker and Stella.

It's almost night but the sun is still able to backlight the blue-black hills against a slightly lighter sky. I am taking a shortcut off Route 23, down a country road; there does not seem to be soul for miles around. I am alone, but not lonely. For here, in Kentucky and Virginia, I finally met the Moores.

III

Transitions

A few miles north of the graveyard where Sue and I found Bonnie, Beulah, and Orel's graves lies the tiny village of Wakefield, on Route 23. There, I met another relative, Maggie Moore West who lived on a farm with her husband Eddie. I had learned about her from Cousin Forest in Texas; she was the daughter of Paris Moore, one of my grandfather Booker's brothers. More important, she had known Booker and Stella.

I had learned earlier that my grandmother, Stella Gambill, was born about 1876 in Lawrence County, Kentucky. Her lineage has been traced back to her 4g grandfather, Martin Davenport, born in 1690 in Virginia. The family later moved down to North Carolina before heading to Kentucky in the mid-19th century[26]. They appeared to be a family of property and substance, probably thinking they were several cuts above the Moores.

Did Stella know about Booker's children? In the hamlets and hollows of eastern Kentucky, it would seem hard to keep secrets like that. It is also tempting to believe that it was the reason that her parents were against the marriage. In fact, they disowned her, according to Maggie. Booker and Stella's wedding, however, took place about 1897, and they had four sons and two daughters – all "B's" – Bonnie, Bruce, my father Bill, Bernard (nick-named "Dude), Beulah, and Booker, Jr. (or "June"). All were born in Kentucky.

Booker was a railroad car repairman between 1908 and 1915 in Fullerton, Kentucky[27]. He then moved his family across the Ohio River to a log cabin on Owl Creek Road, outside Wakefield. Maggie and her son Ted were not sure of the date – perhaps around 1915 – but Ted remembered seeing the cabin before it was torn down.

Maggie's recollections provided a framework for what others told me. Orel and Gene had sent me a photo of Booker and Stella taken probably around 1915 at the county fair in Lucasville, just down the road from the Owl Creek cabin. Although the pose is informal, their

---

[26] Thanks to the research of John Donohew.
[27] Portsmouth City Directory, 1908-09; 1914-15.

expressions are not. Booker liked the hills (and his jug) while Stella liked the city life. Gene Moore remembers his mother telling about an incident when the World War I soldiers were returning home by train. One of the veterans received an unusually warm welcome from Booker's wife: "Stella hugged and kissed the soldier in front of everyone and Booker just stood by, looking like a fool." Lola Spriggs, Forest's wife, described Stella as "pretty wild … with a string of boyfriends. She bought a car for one of them."

In 1917, the Moores moved to Portsmouth. My father transferred to Garfield School's 7th grade at the age of 13 and Booker continued to work in the rail yards for the Norfolk and Western. He took out a mortgage on a house, suggesting some attempt at a stable home life, but it lasted only a year. After selling the house, his family moved around town about as often as my mother's family.

By the 1920's, the family was clearly dysfunctional. Not only did Gene not know about my father; neither did Maggie West, although she knew Junior, Bernard, and Bonnie quite well. The years in California seemed to have erased any memory of Bill. Bruce apparently left the household as soon as he was old enough to strike out on his own. When in later years, Dude visited Bruce at his home in Pennsylvania, Gene recalls that he was embarrassed by the shabby way his father treated his uncle.

Stella and Booker Moore, ca. 1915

By the time Bill and Dude reached high school, they had become football players. Bill was a reserve back for the Trojans in 1922-23, but when several players were injured, the *Portsmouth Times* opined: "W. Moore probably will get a chance to perform at that position. Moore is small but is brimful of nerve and is a sure tackler. He made a good showing the few minutes he was in the game last Saturday [against Ironton.]" The column went on to say that he "was to have been worked at half, but with the new shift in players, 'Dude' Moore would play the quarterback position."[28]

Dude seems to have been the more favored of the two, but took himself out of action for two weeks by running his arm through a window at school while horsing around with another fellow. The cut required six stitches to close.[29]

Bill Moore, 1923

Whether Dude's mishap was the reason or not, "Another change has been made in the backfield this week. Will Moore has been sent to half."

---

[28] *Portsmouth Times,* 19 Oct 1922.
[29] *Ibid.,* 17 Nov 1922.

Portsmouth ran a single wing offense, but in keeping with the style of play that was fashionable then, the team concentrated on defense, waiting for the opposition to make a mistake which it might convert into a score. Since there were only about 15 men on the squad, players went both ways and played either 12- or 15-minute quarters. For someone as small as Bill Moore (5'7", 140 pounds), it meant tackling people who were several inches taller and 50 or 60 pounds heavier. It had to have been punishing to play defense; offense was hard enough. Although he was fast, he could not avoid his share of tackles, blocks, and hard knocks from bigger and heavier opponents.

The 1920's was the decade of sports heroes, particularly in football. Sportswriters like Grantland Rice were creating legends (and metaphors) that still exist. Local sportswriters were trying to emulate the professionals. Knute Rockne, The Four Horsemen, Pop Warner, Red Grange, Bronko Nagurski, and George Halas were all household words, along with the legendary Jim Thorpe, who, in the twilight of his career, played in Portsmouth for the semi-pro Shoe-Steels in 1927. In Portsmouth, football was king. As late as the 1950's, the high school yearbook was reminding its readers – even if in fun – that:

> Ya gotta be a foot-ball he-ro
> To get a-long with the beau-ti-ful girrrls ...

The Ohio River towns of Portsmouth, Cincinnati, Ashland, Huntington, and Ironton (home of the hated and dreaded Tanks) were a significant part of the beginnings of semi-pro and professional football. These games, played on Sundays and sometimes Wednesdays, were, along with the high school games on Saturday, an integral part of a community's pride and self-image. That self-image was apparent at the banquets that the local businesses threw for the teams, some of which were attended by Bill and Dude. The team would be praised for "clean and manly competition, exemplifying the best traditions of the sport".

There was another incentive: the chance for a few – very few – players to get off the treadmill of poverty or semi-poverty and achieve something better than a life in the shoe factories, railroad yards, or steel mill. That window of opportunity was indeed small but then, as my family would say, ten per cent of something was better than 100% of nothing.

Ironton's Board of Education subsidized the semi-pro Tanks by hiring its coach Shorty Davis as athletic director and coach of the high school eleven. Ironton's businessmen also anted up, apparently not worried about compromising the high school's standing as an amateur team. Portsmouth was not so blatant but did follow a similar pattern.[30]

What motivated my father? Was it the desire to find out "Just how good *am* I?" or "What am I capable of?" Whether he had hopes of making it in the pros, or whether he and Dude just liked to mix it up with the boys in the tradition of the mountains, it was a way for players like Bill Moore to prove themselves to others despite their small size. Whatever his reasons, he was a fierce competitor. In the game against Lancaster,

> Moore made 2 when he hit the line … Moore, 3 yards … Moore 6 yards … Moore gained 3 … Moore made 3 … Moore gained 4 … Moore made a gain . Moore gained 2, enough for a first down

He was just getting warmed up.

> W. Moore gained 12 yards around end … and then W. Moore made 10 more. "Dude" Moore made 4; W. Moore made 3 and first down … W. Moore made 5 yards, putting the ball on the visitors' 20-yard line …[31]

In the final game that year, Bill started at right half and made "big gains, one of which was a 37-yarder after intercepting a pass." It was the longest run of the game. He caught another that got the ball to Columbus North's 35-yard line, and he slid off-tackle for a yard. Then, he "was laid out for a few moments as a result of the play, but continued in the game." [32] Such scrappiness promised a bright future the following year.

'Way to go, Dad. Now, I know where I got my hard-headedness. Did you have a Cherokee Knot?

---

[30] Carl M. Becker, *At Home and Away: The Rise and Fall of Professional Football on the Banks of the Ohio, 1919-1934* (Athens: Ohio Univ. Press, 1998), ch. 5.
[31] *Portsmouth Times,* 19 Oct 1923.
[32] *Ibid.,* 30 Nov 1923.

In 1924, however, Booker walked out on his family and moved to Ashland, Kentucky. Bill, who was 21, went with him. Why he gave up his final year at Portsmouth to play football for one of Portsmouth's arch-enemies is a mystery. Was life at home that terrible, or did he just like the relative independence of living with his father?

My mother dropped out of Portsmouth High School with only one semester to complete before graduating. Why? She had enrolled in the commercial-secretarial program her freshman year and her grades were reasonably good[33]. Her family certainly would have needed the income that her bookkeeping job at Union Store and later a cashier's job at Lewis Furniture provided. That would easily have taken precedence over a diploma.

Booker went to work with his brother Paris in the Kentucky-West Virginia oilfields. The terrain there was so rugged that the only way to get equipment into the area was by teams of oxen. Since the beasts were rather touchy about being shoed, they had to be held immobile in large slings, so that Booker could drive the nails into their hooves. A picture of Booker and Paris shows them driving a team of 10 oxen, hauling a gigantic boiler to run the oil pumps in the field. Ted West, Maggie's son, explained that the boiler would be connected to drive rods that ran several pumps at the same time. The oil was then piped to refineries at Ashland.

While Booker was in the oilfields, Bill was having a successful year at Ashland High, although he was smeared for no yardage at all in the game against Portsmouth. His old teammates evidently remembered all his moves. The yearbook listed his favorite sport as "going home for week-ends" (to Portsmouth) suggesting a certain ambivalence by Bill about his parents. The yearbook also predicted that he "probably will land in Hollywood," an uncanny forecast that nearly came true but not for the reasons assumed by the editors.

As for Booker and Stella, she was calling herself a widow by 1930 even though my grandfather was far from dead. Had she and the children been too embarrassed to admit that he walked out on them? Was she so bitter that she wished him dead? Gene Moore recalls that his father Bruce went to Kentucky to try to persuade Booker to return

---

[33] Portsmouth High School, Principal's Office Records.

57

to Portsmouth, but to no avail. He had "taken up" with yet another woman.

When he finally died in 1945, Booker Moore was three weeks shy of his 74th birthday. Aaron wrote on the death certificate that Booker's wife was deceased, but she was not. Booker's obituary said two days earlier that he left "a wife and a number of children together with many relatives and friends in this section" but mentioned no names.[34] Was Aaron exacting some kind of revenge for his brother? More likely, the discrepancies over the death certificate and obituary were a sad recognition that these two people had drifted so completely apart that they had nothing more to say to or about one another, even unto death. Each had been dead to the other for a long time.

Meanwhile, Stella had gone to live in Pennsylvania with Bruce and his wife Nellie, but she had begun to behave erratically. She was obsessed by the idea of returning to Portsmouth and became no longer responsible for her actions. Gene remembered when she crawled out of the house and across the yard on her way to Portsmouth, 150 miles downriver. She was committed to the Woodville State Hospital in 1942 and died there seven years later. Although Gene explained Stella's dementia as a result of her having had typhoid fever, another family member was less charitable; Stella was "just plain mean."

By 1926, Bill was back in Portsmouth to play semi-pro football with the Portsmouth Presidents but was not successful. The season started out promisingly; the *Times* predicted that "Moore will take his turn at quarter[back] with [Jake] Shields." But later, it appeared that Shields had a lock on the job because "his weight gives him an advantage over Moore for the post." Bill rode the bench for a month, getting into only three games, including the final one with the Cincinnati Friars, but only after the Presidents had a big lead. He got a touchdown and an extra point, but the score was 31-0. His small size had finally caught up with him, and no amount of competitive spirit would overcome it, not in pro ball.[35]

The following year, the Presidents became the Portsmouth Shoe Steels (with Thorpe) and then the Spartans (without him). By then, Bill Moore was out of the game. Semi-pro ball was evolving into professional full-time football and being run like a business. The

---

[34] Paintsville, KY, *Herald*, 8 Feb 1945.
[35] *Portsmouth Times*, 23 Oct, 30 Oct, and 22 Nov 1926.

Portsmouth Spartans joined the National Football League in 1931. They were playing – and beating – teams like the Packers, Giants, and Bears. In those days, pro football fans knew where Portsmouth was. In 1933, the Spartans came within a few points of beating Chicago for the NFL championship. Although they were one of the best teams in the league, they could not draw large enough crowds at home and began to lose money. A group of Detroit businessmen bought the Spartans in 1934, gave them new team colors, and renamed them the Lions. An era had passed for Portsmouth, and not just in sports. The city's commercial spirit and its civic brightness and vitality, epitomized by its football, had reached their zenith and had begun to plateau.[36]

On March 29, 1929, Bill and Helen were married before the Rev. J. W. Greenwood of Catlettsburg, Kentucky. Their good friends Charlie Knauss and Mary Elizabeth Willey (who later married each other, then divorced) stood up with them. They settled in the Lincoln apartments in the east end of Portsmouth. Bill worked at the steel mill, while Helen continued her job at Lewis Furniture.

During this time (1929-1933) my father purchased a small pocket dictionary in which he recorded his weight (140 lbs.), height (5 ft, 7-1/2 in.), shoe size (7-1/2), collar size (15), and hat size (7-1/8). His car was a Ford; his watch, an Elgin; his physician, Dr. Bermot; and his hospital, General. Such careful, almost minute, tabulation, along with a precise writing style and clear penmanship reveal something about Bill Moore's character and values. He had an orderly mind and paid attention to details.

His dictionary contained much more than the definitions of 40,000 words. It laid out rules for proper conduct, manners, and etiquette that epitomized the self-improvement ethos of the 1920's: "Every day in every way, I am getting better and better." Here, in one slim volume that could easily fit into a vest pocket, was all the information that an ambitious young man needed to succeed. It showed how to calculate numbers rapidly, drive a car properly, and chair a meeting. There were rules on how to pay a social call:

---

[36] In 1928, Bill's youngest brother, June, entered Portsmouth High School and had a successful athletic career. He lettered in football, basketball, and tennis, was class president his sophomore year, and earned the nickname "big shot" because in the final second of the 1931 state championship game, he sank the winning basket.

Remove your overcoat and overshoes upon entering the drawing-room, but retain your hat and cane if making only a short call... Always let ladies, seniors, and superiors be the first to offer the hand. Do not lounge, tip back in your chair, or sit cross-legged. Do not use the piano or organ without being invited to play.

There were rules for the dining room:

Eat with the fork or spoon, not with the knife. Eat soup from the side of the spoon, not from the end. Keep the elbows close to the side and off from the table. Give to the lady at your side your first attention, whether you have been introduced to her or not. Address servants quietly. Eat slowly and with no unnecessary noise, as sipping, smacking, snuffing, coughing, or sneezing. Keep the feet quiet, and from coming in contact with others.

This was a far cry from Flat Gap or Owl Creek. As for proper conduct on the street:

A gentleman walks at the left of a lady companion except when walking at her right would shield her from crowding; and when passing through a crowd, he should precede and open the way for her. In changing sides, the gentleman should pass behind the lady.
No lady should take the arm of two men at the same time, but a gentlemen may take a lady on each arm. Two gentlemen accompanying a lady should allow her to walk between them.

Keep step... Do not ask questions of non-officials or transients.

There was a specific rule of behavior for almost any occasion, but for anyone who missed the point, there was this final admonition:

There is no great, no small, in right and wrong. Whatever is wrong if done to a thousand men, is wrong if done to one; and whatever is wrong when carried to its ultimate end is no less wrong in its inception.

There is no injustice in respecting the rights of the few, though it displeases the many; but to please the many at the expense of the few, is a great injustice to the few ... 'It is better to be beaten in right than to succeed in wrong.' Have principles of right and then live by them.

'Do right though the heavens fall'.

Quaint? Perhaps. But what did all these rules essentially mean? Were they not trying to convey the virtues of constancy, civility, and respect for others?[37] When Bill combined these qualities with the ones that he learned on the gridiron – determination to succeed despite the odds and taking your share of hard knocks without complaint – he assumes more texture and character. These were qualities on which he would soon have to rely heavily.

By 1933, the Depression had driven Bill and Helen to San Gabriel, California, where he worked as an oil company salesman in Long Beach. Whether or not he had developed tuberculosis before moving out West, he was an invalid by 1936, and he had to quit his job that August. In a letter that he wrote to Maude in November, he described his "pet ailment" but hoped that he might be admitted to Olive View Sanitarium if his X-rays showed enough improvement to warrant treatment. It was now his turn to confront the Curse.

In that letter, Bill also spoke of Helen with love and gratitude: "She's as trim and active as she was at seventeen," but he did not say if she was working outside the home. She would have had her hands full looking after her husband yet they would have needed the income that her secretarial skills could provide. He asked about Callahan and about Helen's siblings. He appeared to feel closer to Helen's family than to his own. In late January 1937, Bill entered Olive View TB Sanitarium, but not before Helen and he ensured continuation of the family name. After seven years of marriage, she became pregnant.

Olive View

Tuberculosis was the leading cause of death in the U.S. in the early 20th century and there was no effective cure. When railroad connections with the East were completed in the 1920's, Los Angeles County was inundated with patients who would go directly to the

---

[37] Both my grandmother and cousin said that Bill Moore kept the dictionary in his bathroom and would study it several minutes each day.

county hospital from the train station, hoping that southern California's warm, dry climate would help them.

To alleviate the pressure of so many who sought treatment, Olive View opened in October 1920, and it was state of the art for that era. Built on the "cottage plan" developed by Dr. Edward Trudeau in upstate New York in 1885, it was intended to provide a pleasant, open-air environment along with absolute bed rest. This, plus pneumothorax treatments that collapsed the lung in order to "rest" it, along with ultra-violet exposure, were the only procedures available at the time. Sometimes, surgeons removed a bleeding lung, but that was only a palliative measure. It was also important to encourage positive thinking because if there were a cure, it often took years to achieve. During such times, patients were isolated from their families and had to endure personal tragedies. Bill Moore was among them.

Olive View became the largest sanitarium in the western U.S., growing to over 1,100 patients and 150 buildings by 1941. Not everyone had welcomed its beginnings, however. In 1917, a wealthy property owner next door objected strenuously to his new neighbor's planned presence. George Thresher complained to the Los Angeles County Supervisors that the only right-of-way available to his property would have to go through hospital grounds. This was simply unacceptable:

> To be obliged to pass through a tuberculosis settlement to reach our homes would be extremely depressing, disagreeable, dangerous, and annoying. It would certainly depreciate the value of our property very materially, if it did not make it wholly unsalable.
>
> Considering it a menace to our health, our happiness, and also an injustice to depreciate the value of our homes, we respectfully request you gentlemen to consider this, our protest, against the selection of this location for the building of a sanitarium for comsumptives[38] .

Thresher fairly spat out the word "consumptives" as though he were describing a leper colony. Fortunately, his objections and the stigma and fear they reflected were overcome. Today, Olive View celebrates "Home-Coming Day" when former patients – now quite

---

[38] 16 Aug 1917. *In* Olive View Archives.

elderly – return, greet the staff and current patients, and celebrate their recovery.

Olive View Sanitarium, Sylmar, California, 1930s

Along with the need for buildings was the need for a clear statement about what was expected from the patients. Dr. William H. Bucher, an early superintendent, minced no words:

> Anyone with Tuberculosis faces a great battle, yet Nature compensates in this as well as in all things, and she tells each and everyone engaged in that struggle that self-preservation is the first law... It is useless to complain and rebel against restrictions and rules originated only with the idea for your welfare.
>
> Apply your intelligence so you can adapt yourself to the problem of getting well. This will lead to the road where you can whole-heartedly 'take the cure'. Courage of the highest order is needed, BUT IT CAN BE DONE, AND IS BEING DONE. WHERE THERE IS A WILL THERE IS A WAY.
>
> Perhaps in some inscrutable way Tuberculosis has a function of preparing the souls of certain men and women for some higher purpose in the Universe... I have seen certainly more patience, courage, self-denial, and unselfish devotion to others in tuberculars than I have noticed in the majority of human beings...
>
> You are therefor, each and every one of you, preparing yourselves for greater things than you realize, and the best that is in you should be given to the effort, and then whether you get well or not does not

> matter for in the striving you have put yourself in touch with the infinite ... something worth more than life itself[39].

These were brave words, but doctors and patients realized that they did not have much more going for them. Inner qualities would be needed. It could be likened to one of my father's football games where the opponents were bigger and heavier. This time, however, the game was for keeps.

Dr. Bucher broadcast his remarks over the campus radio station, which was an integral part of the community that he was forging. The sanitarium also had its own library, chapel, post office, and barber shop. It grew most of its own produce and boasted hog and chicken ranches. Most of the hospital staff lived on campus and provided educational services, occupational therapy, and work programs for patients against the day that they might be cured and discharged. The annual report for 1936-37 noted that only 94 patients out of 1,000 died that year, a little over nine per cent and definitely lower than the national average, giving credence to the idea that prolonged bed rest did work. Those with minimal severity stayed an average of 395 days, while worse cases stayed an average of 591 days[40].

During the 400-plus days he was there, Bill Moore kept a diary for two months – from February when he was hopeful about his recovery until the eighth anniversary of his marriage. He tells of the painful treatments and of much loneliness. He looks forward to Helen's weekly visits and does not refrain from telling his diary how he felt about her:

Ward 103, Olive View Sanitarium
Olive View, California
1937

Sun. Feb. 14 St. Valentine Day & the rain is pouring down. Wonder if she will come? — She arrived at 3:45. Delayed by drowned-out motor. Much trouble. – I can't express my feelings when she came in to the ward. Wonder if she knows how much I love her?

Mon. Feb. 15 A Wild screaming wind swept the sky clear of a few intruding clouds and gave us a beautiful dawn. There's a champagne

---

[39] Radio script dated 7 Dec 1931. *In* Olive View Archives.
[40] 18th Annual Report. *In* Olive View Archives.

tang in the air – and I've got the appetite of a bear. Bring on the coffee.

Had eye, ear, nose & throat exam today. Trouble in throat – hope it isn't TB. Probably be transferred. Was told would [receive] Pneumo[thorax treatment] next Mon. – must be successful – damn important. Will write Helen. God love her.

Tues. Feb. 16 Another beautiful day. Feel fine – Wind is still blowing. Washed my hair today. Boys that took Pneumo are plenty sick – my turn comes Mon.

Wed. Feb. 17 Weather is perfect. A fine breakfast – golly! That coffee is most welcome. My first treatment today for my throat. Ultra Violet Ray treatments for the throat is the latest thing. Hope I get a letter from H[elen]. You know it's hell to be nuts about a girl when you can't be with her.

Thu. Feb. 18 Had a letter from Helen this morn. & the day has been filled with pleasant memories. Two new patients today. One Mexican and one Am.

"Calling All Cars" is on the radio tonite and mustn't miss it.

Fri. Feb. 19 It's another sunny morn – bright and crisp. Had another throat treatment today. Slept thru rest period and had fitful dreams.

Well, my friends, another day is about done – only one more day, then, Helen.

Sat. Feb. 20 Snappy and cold this morn – and a clear blue sky. Ate hearty breakfast and feel tops.

Sat. nite 7:30 – Wonder what she's doing tonite. Glad she's staying with Clarks – damn fine people. I miss our Sat. nite Cinemas & thick malts. But cheer up. She'll be here tomorrow.

Sun. Feb. 21 Sun. morn and blessed with a lovely day. The boys are cheerful on Sun. morn, since the Visitors Ban has been lifted.

Gained my usual lb. Weight now is 126 lbs. Helen came looking like a million – new outfit from head to toe. I find it difficult to keep my hands off her.

Mon. Feb. 22 Had my first Pneumothorax treatment today. Breath is mighty short and pain is getting worse in left chest. Orders not to raise shoulders off bed – must lie in one position. The nurses are very attentive.

Tue. Feb. 23 Breath is still short this morn. Went for Pneumo again but fluoroscope showed a partial spontaneous. Chest is sore.

Wed. Feb. 24 Sick

Thu. Feb. 25 Sick

Fri. Feb. 26 Fluoroscoped again today but no air.

Sat. Feb. 27 Feel pretty good today – think I'll live.

Sun. Feb. 28 Helen came again today and brought me much cheer. There's a terrible letdown when she goes home.

Mon. Mar. 1 Pneumo again this morn – took 400 cc's Sure tight in the chest. Am permitted to use wheel chair, which means I can smoke again.

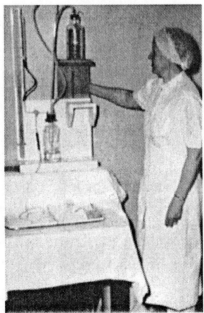

Pneumothorax Machine, 1930's
(Photo courtesy of Dr. Selma Calmes, Olive View)

Tue. Mar. 2 Sick – sick as hell tonite. Had 3 Drs. & head nurse took me down to fluoroscope – wanted to pack me in ice. Gave me hypo and so to sleep.

Wed. Mar. 3 Feel good this morn & hungry as heck – the Dr. is baffled. They've put me on liquid diet. Oh! My! I'm hungry. But Helen is due today – that will help.

Thu. Mar. 4 Back to a gen. Diet & am I glad. Still a bed patient. No smokes.
Man, oh! Man!

Fri. Mar. 5 Fluoroscope again today – but no air. Still a stretcher patient. Well, patience, they tell me, has its own reward.

Sat. Mar. 6 Thank Heavens I can go to the bathroom in the wheel chair again. It was refreshing to smoke again.

Sun. Mar. 7 6:00 P.M. Helen didn't show up & I'm terribly worried. She hasn't called to explain & I'm nervous as hell. I hope she's OK whatever the trouble might be. It's plain hell to lie in bed listening for footsteps that don't appear. It's going to be tough until I hear from her.

Mon. Mar. 8 Pneumo day again Boy! Oh boy! I got a bilateral today – my chest feels like it will burst. Short breath and ripping pains of misery. Can't move my arm. Can't move anything.

Tue. Mar. 9 What a night! I wouldn't attempt to explain the pain. My breath is very short today – but last nite it was terrible. The fluoroscope showed a complete spontaneous. It's no wonder I suffered. My lung is collapsed as far as it will go. But only temporarily, I hope. They've kept me full of hypo's – feel pretty drunk most of the time.

Wed. Mar. 10 Feel better, but still dopey. Helen came again today and was her usual cheerful self. She is a wonderful stimulant and a swell girl.

Thu. Mar. 11 Am still a strict bed patient, but feeling much better. I would give a horse for a good smoke.

Fri. Mar. 12 Fluoroscoped but no air. Am beginning to eat again.

Sat. Mar. 13 They've moved the old gang to their separate wards and a new gang has come to take their place. I'm still here for the time.

Bill Moore and Miss Naut, May 1937

Sun. Mar. 14 Helen came to see me again today. She's gaining weight and looks fine.

Mon. Mar. 15 More Pneumo today and I wonder if one ever becomes accustomed to that needle.

Tue. Mar. 16 Dr. wants me to stay in bed the bal. of the week.

Wed. Mar. 17 My sweetheart was here today and left her presence which lingers from day to day.

Thu. Mar. 18 Another day finds me most grateful. One gets the blues and restless occasionally but all in all, things are pretty good and life is still beautiful.

Fri. Mar. 19 Fine weather but rain predicted. Hurrah! The Dr. gave me permission to use the wheel chair – now for a good smoke.

Sat. Mar. 20 Sat. nite – a big nite in days gone by, but that's becoming ancient history. 8:30 to bed for me.

Sun. Mar. 21 Helen came with lovely flowers, chewing gum & candy – but most welcome was her smile.

Mon. Mar. 22 Pneumo today and was told I had some fluid on left lung. Am to take light treatments for my throat.

Tue. Mar. 23 Dr. Winter informed me I'm to be moved to 105 with the first opening. I hope I haven't T.B. of the throat.

Sun. Mar. 28 Easter morn – always a beautiful morn. Everybody's happy – the weather's fine – the birds seem to know it's Easter. Helen was here and looked very sweet in her new outfit. She's a great inspiration to me. God, Bless her.

Mon. Mar. 29 A cloudy morn. 'Twas also a cloudy morn 8 yrs. Ago – yes sir, I was married – 'Twas in Catlicksburg [sic] Ky. – and the rain was pouring down. Charlie, Mary – Helen & I – I was sober, too.
C. & M. are divorced – much water has gone down to the sea & and we have had many reverses, but I love her the same as eight years ago.

The entries ended although Bill had another 13 months to live. The diary is free of self-pity, anger, or fear. He spoke of what and whom he wanted to live for rather than what he was to die from.

His only other legacy was a wallet that he had made while in occupational therapy. In it, he placed this note to Helen, who was expecting their baby soon:

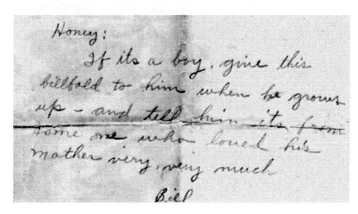

69

Bill wrote once more to "Mother Smith" in March 1938, six weeks before he died. It was, he scribbled, only the second letter he had written back East in two years. He had been a flat bed patient for 11 months and had to use a wheelchair even to go to the bathroom. His weight was down to 105 pounds; the treatments had ended because they had failed. He had not seen Helen for nine weeks because the car had broken down and she could not afford bus fare from San Gabriel, 30 miles away. She was, furthermore, having health problems of her own; "her leg was bothering her again," he wrote with typical understatement.

He added that "I have great faith in my recovery," but he had long known otherwise. It was the Columbus North game all over again when he was knocked out that afternoon a decade and a half earlier but had gotten back up and carried the ball some more. Still "small, but brimful of nerve," he simply would not quit. He thanked Maude for offering shelter to Helen and "the Baby". Then he concluded: "Tell all the folks hello and maybe some day I can come back home."

It was his farewell.

Ward 103, Olive View Sanitarium

IV

Interim

After Bill died, Helen brought their son Michael "back home" to Portsmouth to live with Maude and to find a job. She was rehired by the Lewis Furniture Company, 33 days and 3,000 miles after her husband's death. She stayed there until June 1940, when her boss and good friend, Pete Warsaw, had to let her go because there was not enough work for her. The Depression still held Portsmouth in its grip.

She returned to Los Angeles later that year but only for a few months. Did she intend to retrieve Bill's ashes, to find work, or to pick up some thread of her former life? Whatever the reason, she soon left – without Bill's ashes – and went to Detroit, where she met a salesman, Bryant Albert "BA" Sangston, of Toledo about 1942. They went to Los Angeles and married in 1944 after his divorce from his first wife became final. I stayed with Maude, however, until I went off to college, but Helen wrote and sent money home every week for my upkeep. She and BA came East about every second or third year. Once they took me with them to Florida for a vacation but I remember very little of it. In fact, I remember very little of them. Strangely, I did not question this arrangement and did not fathom the reason for it until many years later.

Between visits, Helen and Bryant wrote my grandmother and me about trips to resort areas, horseback riding and nightclubbing with their friends, and outings to the beach. They sent pictures of their apartment on West 75th Street as well as the neighborhood. During his seven-year stint as stepfather, BA (who had two daughters by his previous wife, plus grandchildren) wrote long letters to his new stepson. He was on the road a great deal and gave long and detailed descriptions of the places he visited – mostly in California and the Far West, but sometimes from places further east. In his letters, he never talked down to me but assumed that I was a curious kid who wanted to know about names and places and how he and my mother lived, worked – and played.

Thus, my grandmother – a half-century older than I – served as both mother and father. Her child-raising philosophy was that of a mother bear watching over her cub. She had a quick temper and one of the fastest backhands in Portsmouth, but woe befell anyone who messed with her grandson. Once in the first grade, the school principal paddled me for fighting on the playground after school. Normally, that would have earned me another paddling at home. I had, however, gone home before returning to the schoolyard, which meant that I was no longer subject to the school's discipline. When Maudie learned what happened, she stormed into the school; the teachers scattered like quail and Mr. Roney learned a new definition of hell on wheels. She was an advocate of tough love, long before that term was invented. But her love was total and unconditional, until her mind began to unravel.

By 1950, Helen's letters and checks had slowed to a trickle and then came to a complete stop by 1953. She and BA had divorced, she had been in an auto accident soon after, and the combination of the two had left her in bad physical and emotional shape. A barely legible letter from her in 1950 was full of despair and loss. Helen's sister Anne recalled later that Bryant had announced the divorce by walking into their apartment with another woman, introducing her as his wife-to-be. In a later letter, Helen sounded more coherent and hopeful that she could get back to work following her recuperation. That was the last I heard from her. It was as though she had vanished. Whether Maude learned something else and withheld it from me, I'll never know; I would not have put it past her.

My father's brother Dude visited my grandmother and me sometime around 1950. I suspected that all the Moores – except Bill – were on her Black List; her coldness toward Dude would have matched his brother Bruce's. She excoriated Dude and his siblings for not caring enough about their nephew even to ask about me for over 10 years. When Dude tried to explain that he had been in the Marines during the War, she did not accept it. Several years later he stopped me on the street to try to explain his position further, but I shied away. He married, and worked a variety of jobs – janitor, driver, and maintenance man – while living in West Portsmouth. He married sometime during the 1950's and died in January 1983. Poor Dude; between Maudie and Bruce, he had a hard time of it. And my attitude was not much better.

With Helen's divorce and her disappearance, and with our estrangement from the Moores, Maudie and I were pretty much on our own. To be sure, her sisters Ruth and Dorothy loved and looked after us, had us to their homes, and were very kind to my grandmother – especially after I left for college. But there was a certain distance. Like the rest of the family, they were somewhat cowed by Maude. She was the one, after all, who raised them and who ruled as the undisputed matriarch. They all were from an era, moreover, that believed that each family should take care of its own problems and not burden others with them. Consequently, I grew up among Maude and her sisters, learning a great deal about the psychology of a generation twice removed from mine. Those lessons stood me in good stead when I became a trustee of a retirement community; I know how that generation thinks. The price I paid, of course, is that I did not learn about my parents' generation.

Although we had to go on welfare after my mother disappeared, Maudie never let on that we were poor. From the time I was 14 or 15, I finished raising myself and marched to my own tune. Maude was always there for me, but I was growing away. She did have her eye on the future, however, and the people of First Presbyterian church – almost a second home – were steadfast in their support. They were as gracious as the New England-style sanctuary where we all worshiped. Rev. Hucksoll had been followed by an extraordinary man, George DeHority, who might have become a father figure except that he was not that much older than I. He was a compelling blend of scholarship, clear thinking, conviction, and compassion. He would have liked me to go into the Presbyterian ministry, but he was too wise to push it. Even so, his impact was broad and deep. The church historian said of him:

> He had come to a church that was divided and unhappy. He left it pulling together, a good, working, witnessing unit. Much of the success he had may be attributed both to his graciousness and sweetness of disposition and to his continuous, thoughtful love for his people. His preaching was always fine and he showed himself the unusual scholar who was able to share his deep thinking in comprehensible terms with laymen… An outstanding quality of his ministry was his prayer life. As only an example, he was rarely at the church that he did not take time to stop in the auditorium and, sitting in his chair as he did each Sunday, look out over the empty pews and pray for each person who sat in them. The church had

reason to feel it had lost a rare gift but to be grateful to have had it for a season.[41]

His people.

Just how extraordinary he was I was not to know until I stopped overnight to visit him and his wife Shirley in upstate New York. It had been nearly 40 years since we had last seen one another, although we kept contact through Christmas letters. Late that night, over his kitchen table, he began to talk about the Portsmouth years and how he had respected my grandmother but kept his distance because he was not sure how she felt about him. He was taken aback when I said she worshiped the ground he walked on and was terribly upset when he left to take another church.

I had asked him if Maudie ever said anything to him about Helen's disappearance; he said no, but agreed that she could have withheld information. Then came his surprise for me. He had told my grandmother back then that she would never have to worry about me if anything ever happened to her. For, in the event of her death, he and his wife Shirley would offer to adopt me as their own son. Maude's protective instincts reared up and she said it would never come to that, but that she appreciated the offer.

I am stunned and overwhelmed; I'll not sleep this night. George and Shirley adopting me? They had three small kids at that time, and very little income, yet they cared that much.

George and Shirley were not the only ones who cared. Mrs. Estella Welty Thompson was a retired schoolteacher who tutored students and gave elocution lessons. Large and imposing, she was a force to be reckoned with, the kind of teacher one might imagine in *McGuffey's Eclectic Readers*. Her demeanor brooked no nonsense, and she had an eye that was the equal of Maudie's in nailing one to the wall, but only for cause. Her husband Isaac seemed about 50 pounds lighter and several inches shorter than she, which gave rise to speculations about who really ruled that household. But I learned that

---

[41] Mary Elizabeth Schwartz, *A History of the First United Presbyterian Church, Portsmouth, Ohio, 1817-1977* (privately printed), 57-58.

her gruffness was mostly for show, and that if she took an interest in a student, she would move heaven and earth for him or her.

I was lucky enough to be one of those students. I was entered in a Prince of Peace oratory contest and also in an essay contest, the "Voice of Democracy." Two of First Church's best assigned themselves as my coaches. Mrs. Thompson was one of them and I spent many evenings in her front parlor on Grant Street practicing for her. Mary Elizabeth Schwartz, who taught creative writing at Portsmouth High and who had been in school with my parents, was the other. They were the kind of teachers who went much further than issuing instructions on phrasing, logic, or pronunciation, although Mary Elizabeth was forever after me to get rid of my Southern Ohio accent. Both women epitomized excellence in all facets of their lives. Both had visions of the world that went far beyond Portsmouth, but that never prevented them from loving that town and its people. They never stopped teaching.

Estella Thompson, however, had another mission – to get me into Wooster. She had graduated from the College in 1912, and had played a role in persuading another PHS graduate – perhaps the best student that the high school ever graduated – to go there in 1919. His name was Howard Lowry; he went on to become president of Wooster and an innovator in American higher education. I was certainly no Lowry – not in any way, *ever* – but Mrs. Thompson saw something in me and was going for a repeat performance 36 years later. We had many conversations, but I was easy to convince. In fact, I had decided on that college in the eighth grade when I attended a youth rally there. There never was any school other than Wooster and there was never any president other than Lowry. Together, they gave me a vision as a teacher of what higher education should be and I returned to that vision time and again.

Wooster's tuition, room, and board, however, came to an astronomical $1,200 for the academic year 1955-56; Maudie's welfare check was $98 per month, and I earned another $42 as a soda jerk in a neighborhood mom and pop store. Even though our rent was only $23 and bread was about ten cents a loaf at Counts' Bakery on Market Street, money was still tight. But I had saved about $600 and Maude was as determined as I about college because the alternatives in Portsmouth were either the shoe factory or the steel mill.

In the 1950's, Portsmouth had not yet realized that it had to construct a new reality. The city was losing its luster and prosperity, along with an increasing percentage of its population. The steel mills and shoe factories, mainstays of the old economy, were soon to be no more. The giant Selby Shoe Company on Gallia Street, which employed over 4,400 workers during the 1940's would eventually become nothing more than a huge vacant lot. The even larger steel mill in New Boston, stretching from city limit to city limit, was to become as distant a memory as Hanging Rock's pig iron furnaces, two generations earlier. A gaseous diffusion plant, built by the Atomic Energy Commission in 1950, did not bring the degree of prosperity that people had hoped for. The end of the Cold War rendered it obsolete. Hard times were returning. Indeed, my grandmother added a Sixth rule to her Five: "When you graduate, leave Portsmouth; there's nothing for you here." Many others evidently were getting the same advice; the city's population by 1990 would be half of what it was in 1950. The city would fight back with the same determination she had when fighting the River for nearly two centuries. It would be a future that in large part celebrated her past – but not yet.

The savings, a couple of scholarships, and several timely gifts from First Church enabled me to finance the first year of college. We did not even think about the second. I had come home to work as a janitor and floor scrubber for the school board that summer when Wooster wrote to offer me a General Motors scholarship. It was a "full ride" for the next three years and paid for everything, minus what I would earn during the summer. The grades of the previous scholarship holder had tanked and he left school. The College needed a replacement PDQ. I was available; besides, President Lowry (and his mother – that's another long story) knew I was from Portsmouth. As a Presbyterian, I suppose I should have believed that it was preordained, but I think just plain luck had a lot to do with it.

After Wooster came four years of graduate study in history at Case Western Reserve University in Cleveland. Of equal importance was the time I spent singing for Robert Shaw in the Cleveland Orchestra Chorus. I covered almost as much choral literature as I did history and from him I got a graduate education in aesthetics. I did not realize at the time what that would mean for my later career as an arts educator and administrator. While the time spent with Shaw does not technically qualify as family history, I took my fathers where I could find them, and he was a great role model. Thus, he belongs in this narrative, because for four years, that Chorus seemed like family.

Interlude

I was but 1/200th of this "amateur" (in name only; we could outsing anybody) ensemble. Shaw, "RS", was also associate conductor of the Orchestra at the time that George Szell – the Heinrich Himmler of University Circle – was conductor, and Louis Lane the other associate. We sang under all three plus whoever of Shaw's proteges – Helen Hosmer, Robert Page, Margaret Hillis, or Ralph Hunter – happened to be in town. Of that latter bunch, Hunter stands out because of a 5-choir, 40-part Thomas Tallis canon that we did for him, spread out all over Severance Hall. The audience had not a clue where to look or listen. Neither did we; we just kept countin' and truckin.'

Shaw once described Beethoven to his collegiate chorale in New York as he was preparing them for a performance of the *Ninth*:

> Beethoven is not precious; he's prodigal as hell. He tramples all over nicety. He's ugly, he's heroic; he roars; he lusts after beauty. He rages after nobility. Be ye not temperate. Enter into his courts on horseback.[42]

The quotation sums up Bob Shaw as well. Where ever he conducted, he left a puddle of sweat on the floor. His blue shirt, buttoned at cuff and collar regardless of the temperature, was his rehearsal trademark. Either he had several dozen or else an active laundress at the Commodore Hotel where he lived. One night he walked into rehearsal wearing a brown shirt; he broke up laughing when we nearly booed him off the podium as an imposter.

Shaw's biographer states that the size of the Chorus depended on how many tenors RS could recruit. Perhaps, but it was the sopranos who could make or break us. We had some screamers in that section who could reach *down* from their skyhooks and wail on those high notes with a brilliance and power that could part your hair. They could be glorious – when they felt like it. In the Verdi *Te Deum* (my

---

[42] Joseph Mussulman, *Dear People . . . Robert Shaw* (Bloomington: Indiana University Press, 1979), 58.

first outing with the Chorus) Shaw had us on more dynamics than a roller coaster. But it was the ending that the sopranos gave to that piece; I can still hear it 40 years later in my mind's ear.

The beginning wasn't bad either. Shaw was adamant about keeping the lid on tight through the *incessabile voce proclamat*, generously giving us an entire eighth rest to get from a triple *pianissimo* to a roaring *sanctus* that lifted the entire audience – even the blasé, black-tie Thursday night crowd that included the reviewers from the *Plain Dealer* and the now-defunct *News* – out of their seats. How we loved to shake them up. By contrast, it was no challenge to get the Saturday night audience with all the college kids excited and yelling. They listened with their hearts, God love 'em. As for Sunday afternoon – *gevalt!* They were family, relatives just off the boat who would loudly applaud the *assistant* concertmaster when he came on stage (tacky, tacky). But they loved the music as much as anyone. Louis Lane conducted a Sunday performance of *Pictures at an Exhibition* that remains the best I ever heard.

Although we had to re-audition every other year to stay in, I can only remember my first. I had just come into town after an all-night party at Wooster where I had stopped to see friends and pick up books en route to Cleveland and graduate school. The dormitory where I was to be a resident counselor was next door to Severance Hall, and as I staggered out of the taxi under my luggage, etc., I was able to see through bloodshot eyeballs that auditions were being held that day, indeed, that very hour. I unloaded my stuff, went to Severance, met RS's incomparable secretary Eddie Burruss, groped my way downstairs to the recital hall, shook hands with Shaw, opened my mouth, and made something come out. I got in.

The following Monday night, however, I died for two and a half hours as I learned for the first time in 16 years of choral singing (starting at age five) what it meant to *work* on a piece of music. Shaw literally did not waste a minute. He was a stickler for detail, especially for enunciation – shades of his Fred Waring days! It was a stitch when we had to learn Catalonian in order to sing Pablo Casal's *El Pesebre*. RS's genius lay in knowing which measure(s) on which to concentrate and which to ignore. Since I could sing either tenor or bass, I became one of about 20 "rovers" whom Shaw used to balance the intonation. We seldom knew which part we would be assigned; it sometimes changed back and forth as he experimented. Although it was a great way to learn a score thoroughly, it was hard to sing and read the music because I wanted to see and absorb every move he made. So much to learn! I remember how he kept his head cocked to one side and his eyes closed – listening. He had great ears.

So did Casals even at age 85 when we sang for him in Puerto Rico in 1962. The occasion was the Pablo Casals Festival and we were in rehearsal when he stopped us to correct a wrong note by the principal harpist of the New York Philharmonic who had come down to play. It was an all-star collection of musicians. Sidney Harth of the Chicago and Alexander Schneider of the Budapest String Quartet shared concertmaster duties. Also present were William Warfield, Maureen Forrester, Juan Jose Castro of Argentina, and a certain South American soprano who had one of the biggest voices – and chests – I had ever witnessed.

Anyway, when Casals corrected the note, the harpist replied, almost worshipfully, "No, maestro; I played it right – I think." "Ah," said Casals almost as a benediction, "but you see, I have very good ears and your note was wrong." End of discussion.

I was a small part of the surprise that Shaw, Schneider, and Casals' wife (now Marta Istomin) sprang on the Maestro, a performance of his *O Vos Omnes* that he had written in 1912 but had never heard sung. We had just gotten off the plane and headed straight for the performance hall at the University of Puerto Rico for our first rehearsal with Casals. He thought we were going to do the Beethoven *Ninth* (practically our theme song by then) but instead, out came this five-part *a cappella* motet that stunned him – for all of three bars. He recognized our little joke and sat back to enjoy it. It was one of the few times we dared not look at Shaw, but then this was history in the making.

Casals then came on stage. Rumors abounded: Good Lord! Was he going to *play* for us? He did not, but he gave us something even better. He began to talk about his days in Spain and his beloved Catalonia. He talked about Franco, the Spanish Revolution, and his resolve to stay in exile until Franco fell. He was dedicating his oratorio *El Pesebre* (The Manger) to the day when peace returned to Spain and throughout the world. This was why he was entrusting his work, his mission, to us when we performed it in San Juan and again in New York's Carnegie Hall on our way home. By the time he had finished, we were so choked up we could not have sung our names.

Actually, *El Pesebre* as a piece of music was not all that great. It was a collection of Catalonian Christmas carols arranged in a nineteenth century romantic style. What sold it was Casals' own humanity and humility. We would be on the risers just before a performance and could glance into the wings to watch his wife place a nitroglycerin tablet under his tongue, make the sign of the Cross over him, kiss him on the cheek, and give him a gentle shove toward the podium. Rather scary. But then, as he conducted, he would get larger and stronger as the music once again pumped life into his small body.

The most magic moment, however, occurred not with Casals, but with RS during a rehearsal of the Schubert *Standchen*, a delicate *lied* that Shaw and Alice Parker had re-arranged for male chorus and contralto. Maureen Forrester was the soloist, a lovely lady who was as gracious as she was talented. The rehearsal, however, was going badly; we were about as *leise* as a hippo in heat. Shaw was mumbling to himself as he conducted – a dangerous sign – and he was about ready to give up (or blow up) when one of our guys said: "Bob, do you think that Miss Forrester could turn around and face us so that we could sing to each other? It might help." RS shrugged. Why not? Nothing else was working. So she turned around. And for the next five minutes...

Plato was *right*. There *is* a Perfection and Purity "out there" that, if we are lucky, very lucky, we just might experience, if but for an instant. I have been There twice in my life, thanks to music. The first time was during the final movement of the Brahm's *A German Requiem* where everything came together perfectly, and the experience was shattering because I did not realize what was happening. But now, I had that extraordinary experience again, this time on a hot, humid stage with RS, Schubert, Miss Forrester, and 50 men with whom I was terribly proud to be associated.

Oh, the power of the music! We were performing "Scenes from *Boris Gudonov*" with Giorgio Tozzi in the title role. When "Boris" came to his hallucination scene and pointed to the ghosts in the rear of Severance, even the Thursday nighters turned around to see if they were there. There was no Platonic transcendence that night or even later when we did three back-to-back performances of the uncut version of Bach's *St. Matthew's Passion*. The experience, however, was just as intense and meaningful.

Shaw and Parker had just completed a new arrangement of the 4-1/2 hour performance work that preserved many of the German idioms by translating them literally. Did it work? By the time we got to the final chorus, "Here Bide We Still" on the third night, I turned around to see half the gang weeping into their scores, exhausted and overwhelmed by the text and music. Nobody had any voice left, but it did not matter. Bach (and Shaw) had taught us the meaning of the Passion. Each of us had reached our personal Good Friday – that moment of introspection and despair when we cry from the depths of our own private hell: "Oh, God, who is so far from me, why must I be so alone? What am I to do?" Answer: You mop up the blood and keep on singing; that's what you do. For, the beat goes on.

Bob Shaw was no saint nor did he pretend to be. One night, we were in Canton to do the Schubert *Mass in G.* Since Szell was not there, the boys in the orchestra felt that they could have a little fun backstage (which in that auditorium was beneath the stage). While Shaw was conducting a chamber piece that used just a few players, the others got up a crap game right out of *Guys and Dolls* to pass the time. With the money flowing freely – those string players really knew how to roll 7's and 11's – somebody decided to provide a little gypsy music for atmosphere. Others joined in and it got so loud *downstairs* that Shaw and the audience could hear it *upstairs*. He could hardly wait until intermission. He was drenched with sweat, his face was as red as a beet, and his voice could have been heard all over Canton. I don't think I had ever seen a display of such rage and unbridled fury, with the possible exception of Iago's soliloquy I saw one night in a Kabuki theatre production of *Othello.*

While his temper could be titanic (going back to the Beethoven quote), RS could also do the *mea culpa* bit when it suited him. "There are no bad choruses," he would softly cry after we had butchered a part for the umpteenth time, "only bad conductors. I've let you down again. I am so sorry, so sorry …" as his voice trailed away. Bull. He knew he was making us all feel guilty as hell for singing so badly and having him bear our crosses. How could we do this to poor ol' Bob who was busting his hump for us? Shades of the St. Matthew and St. John passions, plus a few Mozartian *lachrymosae* to boot! He was as much snake oil salesman and psychologist as he was musician. And we loved it.

Robert Shaw taught me the excitement and beauty of pitch and tempo, that is, precise pitch and tempo. If, to Blake "eternity is an hour," the opposite was equally true to Shaw. It was astounding what he could crowd into a sixteenth note. Since he knew exactly how long a beat was, he knew exactly what to demand of us. And therein, paradoxically, resided enormous artistic freedom.

Similarly for pitch. RS always said that we could sing twice as loud with half the effort if we all sang in tune. He proved it one night, when he literally tuned us in Severance Hall, with its great acoustics (even better after its recent remodeling). As he adjusted our pitches, voice by voice – we were singing in fifths – we could begin to hear overtones that no one was singing. Although we were engaged in elementary physics, the effect was still hair-raising.

Shaw's command of speech was as profound as his mastery of music. He could speak bluntly and profanely in one- and two-syllable words, or he could go hang-gliding with the English language, creating images, allusions, metaphors, synedoches, and metonymies that soared to the outer reaches of the human imagination. Yet, he maintained a down-to-earth quality that proclaimed his connected-ness to all things human. His occasional letters to us ("Dear People …") were as classic in their style as in their content. There, as well as in rehearsal, Shaw would discover the magic of the music once again, as though he were opening a score for the first time and being thrilled by what he discovered. By treating the familiar as unfamiliar, he was able to create freshness, new insight, and – above all – renewal, for himself and for us. It was perhaps his greatest gift.

He was doing the same thing thirty years later when in 1992 he conducted an open rehearsal at Ohio State University with some 700 singers culled from his many choruses over the years. The occasion was as nostalgic and emotional as any alumni reunion. The only change in RS were the Ben Franklin spectacles now perched on the end of his nose. We sang music that some of us had not sung for nearly a third of a century, but with him time dropped away, and we were eager, attentive choristers once more.

When Shaw was installed as minister of music at the First Unitarian Church in Cleveland in 1961, he preached a sermon entitled "Music and Worship in the Liberal Church." It was not a political tirade; instead, it searched for the deeper meaning of words like "worship" and "liberal." Worship, he noted, was defined as "a state of being or growth of a people of worth." He linked that definition with "liberalism" which included the idea of a "free people." By combining the two concepts, RS argued that a liberal church was one that enabled a free people of worth to grow up. It followed then, that all aspects of the worship service – including the music – must promote that concept. That was good advice, not only for the Unitarians, but also for the Cleveland Orchestra Chorus.

We did a lot of growing up with Robert Shaw. He often said to us that we did not have to be great singers to be a great chorus, just intelligent singers. He would take care of the rest. And he did. When he died in 1999, I tried to ease my grief by imagining what rehearsals were now going to be like Up There. One thing for sure: Those cherubim, seraphim, and assembled angelic host would be sweating bullets over enunciation, pitch, and rhythm. And I could imagine the Great Jehovah, pleased as punch, urging him on: *"Go for it, Bob! I've waited an eternity for this sound!"*

Maude

I had been away from home since 1959; Sue and I married and began our family. Each time we visited my grandmother, it was evident that her mind was deteriorating. Her apartment on Front Street – she had finally left Second – was next door to a nursing home that "controlled" its patients – inmates? – by tying them in their lawn chairs so that they could not escape through the gate. It was not foolproof, however, and more than once we could look out the window to see the cops dragging back some poor, wailing, old woman who had broken free. It was not a pretty scene, and my grandmother swore to me that she would rather die than go into "one of those places." It was an oath not to be taken lightly.

Soon after we had visited Maude in August 1966, her sister Ruth called me to say they could no longer do anything for her. While physically healthy for her age, she was becoming abusive and erratic; she refused help from her neighbors and frightened them away. The only alternative was a nursing home. Would I talk to her about that? Ruth did not have the courage to face her and I wasn't too happy about the prospect myself. I drove back down to see her but I'm sure she knew why I was there even before I opened my mouth. I said my piece, and that I would return to help her find a suitable place. She said not a word. The Look said it all: *Et tu, Brute?* She turned and went into her bedroom. I left and drove back to Bowling Green, ready to make arrangements.

Mike and Maude, 1960

No sooner had I entered our apartment than the phone rang. It was Aunt Ruth again. Maudie Gracie – the woman who had written Bill Moore to offer her home to my mother and me and who had raised, punished, loved, and defended me after Helen left – was dead. She was 85. She had been taking Digitalis for years for her heart; Sue suspected that she may have emptied the bottle to make good on her promise never to enter "one of those places." It certainly would have been in character. No one ever told Maude Yates Smith how to run her life.

In contrast to her death, her burial was a hoot. She had left extremely specific instructions about the disposal of her remains – a quick funeral and cremation, followed by burial in her father's grave at the Hanging Rock Cemetery. She never cared much about death and its trappings and had drilled me over the years on what I was to do if I ever came home from school and found her dead. It had become automatic and I was now grateful to her for it.

We had the funeral at Daehler's Mortuary on Eleventh Street. By 1966, the ownership had passed to Harold Daehler, who was about my age. I asked him after the funeral when he might be able to give me my grandmother's ashes. "Gets pretty hot in there, Mick," he observed. "Really can't rush it. Couple o' days should do 'er, though."

In the interim, I finished disposing of the household goods and I chose between the furniture that I wanted to keep or give away. Two days later, I went to collect Aunt Ruth and her husband Earl to take them to the funeral home. When we got to Daehler's, Harold came out carrying the urn and wearing asbestos gloves.

"Yer grandma didn't cool off as fast as I thought," he said, "but she'll be all right by the time yew get to Hangin' Rock. Uh ... could you'ns use a shovel?"

Good idea, I said, and we loaded up – Aunt Ruth and I in the front seat with Maudie between us on a thick towel, and Uncle Earl, a kindly man who was as deaf as a post, in back. Harold's shovel and the furniture filled the rest of the station wagon.

As we drove along the Ohio River, it became increasingly clear that my aunt was very uncomfortable sitting next to this new version of her sister. She kept glancing down at the urn cooling next to her. Trying to think of something to say, she finally blurted out, "Well ... Maudie always did like car rides."

"WHAT SAY?" bellowed Uncle Earl. Further conversation was discouraged.

When we got to the cemetery – which at that time was accessible only by driving on the abandoned railroad bed – we had to climb a steep hill to reach Grandpa Yates' grave. Once there, we had to be careful where to dig, because a year or so earlier, Maudie had gone there with her son Philip to bury his brother Ralph's urn atop Grandpa Yates but they had not marked the spot. I prayed I wouldn't hit him on the way down.

Scenes from *Arsenic and Old Lace* came to mind as I dug through the shale, roots, and clay because I recalled that Uncle Ralph (The Three-Fingered Dove) had died in 1941 but had spent the next quarter-century in Maude's cedar chest in the front room. When I was a small boy, I would rummage around in that chest because I liked looking through all the memorabilia that she had stored there. Every time I came across this strange, attractive copper "can" whose top was held on by two screws that I could not get undone, I would shake it like a maraca, and ask my grandmother what it was. She would get a strange look on her face and bark at me to stop messing up things.

But now, Maude was next to her son and on top of her father, and we headed back to the car to find that it had a flat tire. Not all the railroad spikes had been picked up when the tracks had been removed. Out came the furniture because the spare and jack were underneath. The tire was replaced and we finally ended the day at one of Scioto County's more upscale dining salons, Pop's Truck Stop in Wheelersburg.

No one would have laughed at that day any harder than my grandmother.

The cedar chest is now in our living room.

V

Pilgrimage

Olive View – 62 Years Later

Thirty-five thousand feet over Nebraska and flying at 650 mph through banks of clouds.

Sue is well into David Gergen's memoirs and I am reviewing the invitation we had received from Dr. Selma Calmes, chief anesthesiologist and unofficial historian of the UCLA-Olive View Medical Center in Los Angeles. The hospital was celebrating its 80th anniversary. Would we like to participate?

I had met Selma over the Internet a year earlier when I queried Olive View's web page for information about my father. She immediately responded and over the months we became good friends. I sent her some of Bill Moore's letters plus a transcript of his 1937 diary. Selma said that the diary was the first document the staff had seen that described life at Olive View from the patient's point of view. The diary also touched something deep inside Selma, for she, too, had been on a quest for her past, to the island of Corregidor in the Philippines where she had been born. Her father and grandfather had been career officers in the U.S. Army, and she and her mother were evacuated from "The Rock" shortly before Japan invaded. Like me, she had never known her father because he died in Europe shortly after D-Day. Like me, she sought understanding by returning to her roots.

With that revelation, we became linked in a special way. What would our fathers have said to us? Did we live up to their expectations, hopes, and dreams? Selma had been born into a way of life that had been threatened by the War; mine by the Depression and disease. But our families, encouraging us to go on, had preserved the values of our fathers. In my case, I also received a liberal dose of my grandmother's ethic which reinforced Dad's 40,000-word dictionary as well as his diary: "Pull up your pants, boy, and make something of yourself when you grow up." My father, wiping the mud off his football uniform, would have concurred.

I had not spoken to Selma directly until the day before we flew out. She wanted to clear up some details about the anniversary celebration and gain my approval of them. In addition to the diary transcript, I had sent out some pictures, letters, and parts of the family history narrative that I had completed. She had said simply that she was going to use them as part of a display, if I did not object. Her words "use them" were to become the understatement of the year.

The clouds have given way to a clear afternoon, but another layer paves the sky below us like a cobblestone street. The sun glistens off the starboard nacelle as the plane lurches and then rights itself over the prairie. The Rockies are now visible in the far distance.

If I were asked to "say a few words" at the ceremony the next day, what would they be? I keep thinking about the timing of things. Bill entered Olive View January 28, 1937, not more than a week after he and Helen had conceived me. After seven childless years, why did they want a child just then? Was it a conscious decision? It was the middle of the Depression. Dad's TB had forced him to quit his job the previous August and he was afraid that he might be too sick to be admitted to Olive View; it did not handle hopeless cases. Even so, they knew the odds of his surviving; too many Moores had died of it. I would like to think that Helen wanted something by which to remember her husband. That would be consistent with the love that Bill expressed for her in his diary – a love that kept his memory alive for six decades and now brought us to California to honor them at last.

Selma's husband Bob met us at the airport and then picked Selma up on our way to dinner. Their extraordinary hospitality lasted non-stop for the next six days. They located a motel for us, loaned us one of their cars, took us to dinners, and laid out a full itinerary for our first two days – and we had not yet experienced the best part.

The next day, Sue and I drove the short distance from our motel to Olive View. It is located at the northern end of the San Fernando Valley, spread along the base of the San Gabriel Mountains, and about 50 minutes from downtown LA – that is, if the freeways are not jammed. As we viewed the grounds, we found that the few remaining Spanish mission–style buildings, characterized by red tile roofs and heavy stucco arches with the San Gabriels as their backdrop, would have created a beautiful and serene environment in the 1930's. We quickly concluded that Bill could not have been in a better place to recover – or to die.

We arrived early so that we could meet Selma's staff and spend some time in the hospital archives. We were particularly interested in the 1937-1938 editions of the *Olive View Point,* a monthly newspaper published by the patients. We read news of patient discharges, cures and deaths. The editors discussed new treatment methods and gently teased various staff personnel. There were cartoons and a fair amount of gallows humor. These were people who expected to spend years here, with long hours of absolute bed rest, flat on their backs with no distractions. They needed every morale booster they could devise.

After lunch, Sue and I entered the auditorium for the program and got the surprise of our lives. My father's diary and letters were not only in the display; they **were** the display. Selma had reproduced, enlarged, and mounted them on about ten 24" x 30" posters that lined the walls. There were pictures of Bill in high school and in his football uniform and there was also a picture of my grandmother. There was Helen holding me on her lap in 1938 after we came back to Portsmouth. One poster contained excerpts of the family history I had been writing. To all of this, I added Dad's original diary that I had brought with me; people took their time reading it. Sue and I began to wish desperately that we had brought our children and grandchildren – Bill and Helen's progeny. We simply had no idea it would be like this.

The two-hour program for about 75 people recalled Olive View's history since 1920 and its struggle with earthquakes, fires, financial shortfalls, changing medical practices, and the politics that county commissioners played with the hospital. Speakers paid honor to Dr. William Bucher and his role in shaping the philosophy. Others remembered the 1971 earthquake that had destroyed a new 885-bed facility only four months after it had opened. That disaster nearly closed the place. Dr. Alkon, LA County Health Commissioner, spoke of her mother, Dr. Jane Skillen, who was chief of surgery at Olive View. Dr. Skillen had emigrated from Ireland, graduated from the University of Michigan medical school as a surgeon in 1929, and came to work at Olive View for the next 35 years. She met and married Emil Bogen, another staff physician and they lived on the grounds as they raised their family.

I was called up and presented with a certificate of appreciation for my donation of materials. Selma along with Melinda Anderson, the hospital administrator, also gave me a framed picture of Ward 103, where my father lived. The ward had disappeared among the earthquakes and remodeling, but a photo had survived. I thanked them and started back to my seat, but Selma asked me if I would like to say "a few words." As I returned to the podium, my wife's tears started. I dared not look at her. Grateful for the thinking I had done on the plane, I said (more or less):

> I speak for both Sue and myself when I say thank you for this day. Dr. Calmes, with what I have come to know as typical understatement, said that she was going to have a 'few things' on display. I didn't realize that it was going to be this wonderful of an exhibit honoring my father's memory.

> I have thought a lot about coming here in the months since Selma and I have been in contact. I keep dwelling on the fact that my mother and father had been childless for seven years until a week before Dad entered this institution. It was then that they conceived me. I would like to think that, in the midst of knowing what could happen to my father, they opted for life, and decided that this family was going to survive and endure, come what may.

> There have been Moores in this country for over 250 years, when someone – we think his name may also have been William Moore – lived in Virginia and fought in the Revolutionary War. My great-great-great grandfather Isaac fought in the Civil War until he was bushwhacked by a bunch of Yankees; his grandson, unfortunately, was a deserter from the Confederate Army! I think, though, that John Wesley Moore can be excused for his conduct because he had been married less than a year and wanted to get back to his new bride and more important, to his crops in Kentucky.

> Over a dozen members of my family have died of tuberculosis over the years, including my father's sister in 1930. The disease became known in the family as the 'Moore Curse.' But then, it was a curse that affected so many others in this country until the pioneering work of people like the physicians at Olive View and the discovery of antibiotics began to make a difference.

For that, I am grateful to all of you as I am sure many others are who have benefited from your research and who were spared the ravages of the disease and the breakup of their families. But even though my father was not so lucky, he and my mother did perpetuate life, which has enabled my wife and me to come back and say 'thank you' – to claim his memory and to celebrate our family's name.

By the time the program and reception finally ended, this extraordinary day had seemed to last a lifetime, but it was only 5:00 p.m. So, Sue and I drove to San Gabriel to look for the house where Bill and Helen had lived before he entered Olive View. We had the address – 222 Winchester Place – from his letter to my grandmother. Thanks to Sue's expert navigation, we found the house, a small, stucco duplex now housing a Korean senior health care and exercise center.

We took out Bill's letter that he had written in November 1936 and read it aloud:

> Each evening I go down to the drug store, which is one block down the street, for the newspaper. That is about the limit of my outdoor recreation. Helen serves my meals in bed when I'm not feeling so good. I shave and bathe and listen to the radio so you see I'm getting along pretty good.
>
> I am sitting on the front, which faces the Sierra Madre Mts. – the trees and grass are green – the flowers are in bloom and the weather is perfect – to prove it I am dressed in broadcloth pajamas.
>
> Helen is reading and our dog "Stinky" is asleep in the chair with his feet sticking straight up in the air...

We stood in the gathering October dusk and looked around as we read. Although much had changed, we could see the green mountains and experience the mild fall weather, just as he had described it. We turned around, and saw the drugstore – Perveler's Drugs – on the southwest corner of San Gabriel Blvd. and E. Live Oak Street. It stands near the old San Gabriel mission that had been founded when California still belonged to Mexico. We retraced Bill's steps to the drugstore and chatted with some of the clerks. It had been at that corner for 40 years and for 19 years before that just down the street. It still maintained a mom and pop flavor and even though Mr. Perveler had long been dead, people who came in to pay their utility bills still remembered him. Despite its worn, cluttered look, it projected warmth and community. Bill would have felt welcomed.

The sense of closeness to my father that had begun that afternoon at Olive View was growing. We were now where Helen and he lived and where I had been conceived. I had learned and felt more about them in one afternoon than in the previous sixty years. But could we discover where he was buried? My grandmother had maintained that he was in the cemetery at Lucasville, just north of Portsmouth, but Sue and I were never able to find his grave. If he were still in California, could we somehow bring his and my mother's remains back home, if only symbolically?

Saturday, Selma and Bob took us on an extensive walking tour of Olive View. Encompassing some 600 acres, it had been part of a ranch that formed the grounds in 1920. Age, earthquake, and neglect had destroyed many of the original buildings; others were recently razed, leaving raw scars in the earth. With the help of our imaginations and a 1930 site map, however, we were able to reconstruct in our minds something of the earlier flavor of the place. We tramped the chaparral and arroyos and came to appreciate something of the fragile geology of the San Fernando Valley. We walked through the ruins of the old surgery building and a nurses' residence hall, heavily damaged by the earthquake of 1971 and now almost obscured by untended bushes, trees, and vines. Despite the ruins and overgrowth, we could see the artistry and care of the architects and masons who built them in the 1920's. It was a ghostly celebration of their beauty.

Selma's historical instincts emerged as she and Sue – her willing accomplice – scavenged the place for artifacts that would be part of a museum she was planning. They found a stainless steel water pitcher, dented but repairable, as well as a bedpan that she sent Bob to retrieve – in the manner of all good-natured husbands. There were no artifacts to be recovered at the site of Ward 103, however, for it appeared that the abandoned building on the site had itself been a replacement. But it was enough to be able to stand at the site and photograph it. The tall evergreens, the view toward Los Angeles, and the peace of the place that my father had seen and experienced were still there.

We had borrowed a biography and writings[43] of Dr. Bucher, and in one of his poems he captured something of what Bill and Helen Moore represented:

A Raindrop

My individuality is a little sphere,
A fragment of a cosmos, an entity
Rolling in space to an unknown destiny.
Falling, I splash the earth with my life;
Dying, I give life to a smouldering seed
That awakes, and blesses me in my dying throes.

Dead, shattered in all my parts, I live
In the juices and spirit of a Tree,
From whose leaves I see afar
My father the Sun,
My mother, the Sea.

Helen

While honoring my father, we had also come to Los Angeles to find out about my mother. It was time to shift emphasis. After touring Olive View we headed downtown to see what we could learn about places where she and Bryant had lived and the nursing home where she died.

Helen Sangston, 1946

---

[43] Emil Bogen, ed. Surgeon Errant: The Life and Writings of William Henry Bucher (1935).

Where had she been since 1951? It still was hard to adjust from the old assumptions to the new reality. Was it possible to trace Helen's whereabouts the last three decades of her life? Old newspaper clippings, yellowed letters, and vague memories needed to be re-examined closely. Our prior inquiries had yielded nothing, but if we were "at the scene," as we now were, we might learn something. We knew where Helen and Bryant had lived and we had in hand about five letters that she had written between 1946 and 1950. We also had Bryant's death certificate as well as the name of the woman he married after he had divorced Helen. Sue and I decided to start with the city directories at the LA library to locate the places where Helen had lived after her divorce in 1950. We needed to reconstruct her environment as a context for understanding her better.

The Los Angeles main library is a magnificent place in which to work; its electronic databases and reading facilities are enviable. Even better, the library allows up to three hours of cheap parking in an underground garage – in downtown LA, no less. But we quickly learned how much of an obstacle the city's sprawling and fragmented growth posed. There have been no comprehensive city directories since 1942, and the neighborhood directories were indexed only by street addresses, not by names.

After several hours, we found only one new address in the 1954 telephone directory for Helen – on Figueroa Boulevard – and then gave up for the day to go to dinner with Selma, Bob, and some friends at the recently remodeled Union Station. In 1943, Bryant had mailed me a post card that showed the outdoor waiting room of the then new Station. It had fallen into disrepair but its restoration enabled me to find the exact spot where the picture had been taken. The experience of standing there and taking another picture allowed us to salvage something from a disappointing afternoon.

The next day, however, was more rewarding. The relative lack of traffic on Sunday made it easy to reach the Westlake Hospital where Helen had been a patient from February until her death in October 1984. It was a depressing, rundown place in a squalid part of town; its atmosphere reminded me of the nursing home next door to my grandmother's apartment in Portsmouth. Even though Westlake did not tie its patients into their chairs, it had that same sense of emptiness and sadness. Nearby, cheap rooming houses and weed-choked, littered

Westlake Convalescent Hospital

lots bespoke a neighborhood that probably was not much better 16 years earlier. The chilly, rainy day accentuated the sadness. Since it was Sunday, no administrators were around and the others, despite their courtesy, knew nothing.

Heading south on Figueroa, we reached the address that we had found the day before. We were in the middle of Watts. We quickly took some pictures and continued south. When we turned on West 75th, I had a sense of *déjà vu* although I had never been there before. The photos that Helen had sent home over the years – of their apartment, the street, and the neighboring houses – made the area recognizable, even though the street had deteriorated and the apartment building at 602 had been gutted for renovation.

602 W. 75th St.

We retrieved two letters that my mother had written in the 1940's and read them. As familiar as I had been with them, I had never paid attention to the names of two sets of neighbors that Helen had mentioned. Kay and Lyle lived next door to Helen and Bryant, and Betty and Paul were across the hall. The couples came by each evening to watch TV with Helen when the programming began at 6:30.

Sue and I had the same thought simultaneously: Could we find *them* in the library's databases? After viewing two other homes associated with Helen or Bryant, we drove back downtown to the library and its telephone microfiches. Again, no luck, until Sue's intuition led her to a regional computer data base of 115 million names. There was Lyle, living not too far away. We called – and began to turn the clock back 50 years.

Lyle and Paul had been in the Army together during World War II and were just starting their careers in the dry cleaning business near 602 W. 75th. The Sangstons brought their cleaning to them and Helen briefly worked for Lyle in 1948-49. He recalled the parties – and drinking – that had characterized their relationship with them but could not remember what happened after the divorce; they all had drifted apart. He and Paul still kept in touch and he gave me Paul's phone number.

No one answered, but Sue, who was now on a roll, located one other person on the index – Bryant's third wife, Vivian! She lived in Fullerton, near the last address I had had for her in 1968. That strange feeling – of calling a total stranger and telling her I was part of the family – returned. Vivian, however, sounded delightful, and arranged for us to see her the next afternoon. It had been a good day.

Vivian

Before heading toward Vivian's home, we spent a long morning on the phone; the dam that had held back so much information about Helen began to crack. First was Paul, who gave me a detailed account of his life and his many business activities, but interspersed that with snippets of information that allowed me to get a better picture of the Sangstons. He expanded on Lyle's observation about the parties at the Elks Clubs, the drinking, and behavior that characterized two alcoholic people. He described Helen as "bright, bubbly, life of the party – always had a drink in her hand, but never got out of line." "She drank pretty well but could hold her booze and never went over the edge. She loved everybody." It was a classic and tragic description of alcohol addiction.

I then called the Social Security Administration office in LA, and learned more in 45 minutes than I had in three months of writing letters to them. A kind lady with a Bronx accent as thick as the LA smog but who opened up like Mount St. Helens read me Helen's entire employment record dating back to 1937 – everything. It showed that she seldom worked more than six or eight months at any one place until 1952, when she took what must have been a part-time job for five years at a store in Encino. Her earnings were pitiful. She had to have been receiving public assistance, and we know that she had been on MediCal. There were no Social Security contributions between 1957 and 1967, the year she began receiving a pension of $52.30 per month. By the time she died in 1984, her monthly check had risen to $226 a month minus $14.60 for Medicare payments. Therein arose another mystery: How did Helen support herself for ten years before becoming eligible? The welfare records had been destroyed long ago.

Then it was the Mountain View Cemetery's turn. I had written the company several months earlier but was told they had no information about my mother's cremation or burial. This time, the speaker was able to locate the successor to the company that had handled Helen's funerary arrangements. We were just getting to the interesting part when the cell phone battery began to run down; besides, we were afraid of being late for our appointment with Vivian. I would have to call back later.

As we drove to her apartment, I did not know what to expect or feel. This was, after all, "the other gal" to whom my mother referred when Bryant walked out on their marriage fifty years ago and it was the woman he married the day his divorce from Helen was finalized by a Las Vegas judge. These thoughts, however, were set aside when I met her. Vivian is a spry, alert, sunny, 80-plus senior citizen who lives alone and enjoys life to the fullest. She immediately captivated us. She had worked with Bryant in the drapery manufacturing business but gave that up when he died in 1968. The certificates on her walls, recognizing her many hours of community and school volunteer work, attested to her vitality. She has written over 20 booklets for local elementary school children that she uses to encourage their reading. She told us that she writes poetry and plays pinochle every Tuesday. Her engagement calendar revealed an active social life.

Sitting with her two parakeets, she said she had never met Helen directly, but her tale paralleled Paul's. She knew about BA's and Helen's drinking, and by the time she married Bryant, his had gotten worse: "Some days after getting home from work, he could barely make it from the car to the house." She joined Al-Anon, and began to learn the litany of tough love instead of enabling. Finally, he went to an Alcoholics Anonymous meeting, joined, and stopped cold. That revelation allowed us to play the next, crucial card. Sue asked her if Helen's drinking was responsible for the breakup of the marriage. Vivian emphatically answered, "Oh, absolutely!"

When she brought out a photo album of Bryant's, I saw duplicates of photos I had received years ago of him and places where he had gone. But where were the other photos that were part of the series that they had sent me – the ones of him with Helen and their friends? Where were the photos of the beach, the rodeos, and the horseback riding? Those had been removed, leaving only daubs of dried glue that had once held them to the page. My stepfather had compartmentalized his life quite well.

I asked about Bryant's children by his first marriage, children who had grown up in Ohio, but whom I had been unable to trace. Of course she knew them, said Vivian; she hears from them every Christmas, and she produced the names and addresses of Bryant's two daughters, Phyllis and Shirley, by his first marriage to Nellie. She also had the names and addresses of a profusion of grandchildren and great-grandchildren. She spoke fondly of them as though they were her blood kin. But, she added, Bryant never mentioned that Helen had a son.

There was so much more to ask, but it was getting dark, and we had a long drive up the terrifying freeways to our motel in Sylmar. We took our leave of Vivian, but stopped to get flowers, giving me a chance to say goodbye once more to this gracious lady.

Although we had learned much about Bryant and Helen, we neither had accounted for the three decades she had disappeared, nor had we discovered where she and Bill were buried. Their death certificates said simply that they were cremated, and our plane was scheduled to fly out of LA the next day. I called the County Public Administrator, who is responsible for disposing of the remains of indigent and/or unknown persons. After visiting Westlake Convalescent Hospital, after reviewing her employment history, and after talking with Lyle, Paul, and Vivian, we were quite sure that she fell into that category.

Again, I found someone who listened and wanted to help – how different it was from earlier contacts with City Hall! Bert Langi said that he would need several days to retrieve my mother's file from the archives, but I was to call him when I got home. He explained that when someone dies and is not claimed, the body is taken to the morgue for storage while the court determines whether there is an estate. If there is nothing to be probated, the Public Administrator tries to locate the family. If there still is no claim, then the body is cremated and the ashes are stored for three years. After that, they are buried in a common grave at the county cemetery.

We checked out of the motel in Sylmar and moved to one near the airport so that we could return Bob and Selma's car, say goodbye to them, and depart without having to fight the traffic. After checking in, I called the funeral home to resume the conversation begun the day before. They requested a fax of her death certificate. I sent it, but then they called to say that it was unreadable; something was wrong with the thickness of the paper. I hand-copied the information on another, thinner sheet and tried again. Since it was closing time, however, they said they could not call me until the next day.

Wednesday, less than an hour before we had to leave for the airport, the fax arrived. It was my mother's pre-need, pre-death request that she had signed with the funeral home, directing that she be cremated and her ashes scattered in the Pacific. She paid the cost of the burial – $245 – out of her social security checks. Included were the cost of cremation ($50) and a box of acknowledgement cards ($3). She then signed and dated it, less than four months before she died. Although many questions remained about those 30 years between her divorce and death, we at least knew how it ended.

But then I learned why we did not hear from her. Next to the question asking about her family, she had printed "no known relatives." Those words hit hard. Why had she chosen to die outside her family? Was it despair at her drinking and her divorce from Bryant? Had her self-esteem taken such a beating that she felt she could never go back home? Had my grandmother said something that kept her away? Was she suffering from dementia? Or did she feel that after all these years there was simply nothing to return to, that she was already in effect, dead to her family? I certainly thought she had died long before; perhaps the feeling was mutual. We will probably never know, but it is tragic to consider that she never saw her grandchildren or that we never had a chance to make her last years a little easier – at least to say goodbye. She did list Harold as a friend, who may have lived in the same apartment building as she did. I can only hope that he was there for her at the end.

We boarded the shuttle for the airport still not knowing about Bill. Once again, our genius for recognizing the obvious came to our rescue; the answer had been before us all the time. Bill Moore's death certificate clearly stated that he had been cremated at the LA County Crematory; why not simply call them and ask? Of course, it took several calls to reach the right number and I was advised to let the phone ring – there was only one employee on duty. Craig Garnette finally answered and when I gave him the information, he said, "Give me a minute". That was about all the time we had, as passengers began edging toward the boarding gate. We waited, watching our cell phone steadily lose its charge again.

We were up to the gate when he came back on the line: "Yes, we have your father. He was cremated in 1938 and when nobody claimed the ashes, we buried them in a common grave in our cemetery on First Ave." It was as Bert Langi had predicted. "If you get back out here," Craig added, "I think I can locate the general area for you."

Several months later, Selma sent me a clipping about the cemetery[44]:

> More than 150,000 people are buried beneath its sloping, well-tended lawns, but few visitors ever come to lay flowers on the unmarked graves here, where Los Angeles has buried its dispossessed dead for more than a century...
>
> For several days each December, the cemetery is unusually busy. Only one funeral per year is held there – county employees simply call it "the service". [Clyde Emerson, Craig Garnette, and Albert

---

[44] Lisa Leff, "The People Who ID the Does," *Los Angeles Times Magazine*, 6 May 2001, 19.

Gaskin] are the only mourners, and they gather around Phil Manly, a second-generation county hospital chaplain and interdenominational Protestant minister.

… The county is required by law only to inter unclaimed remains, but the funeral has been a tradition for as long as anyone can remember, a voluntary, albeit imperfect, exercise in decency. "It's still kind of an awesome service for me," Manly says. "I do many individual services throughout the year, but only one like this."

Standing above the final resting place of 2,703 people it's impossible not to ask … "If I die here, will my soul not rest?" Manly attempts to answer it. Raising his voice above a lawn mower and weed trimmer wailing nearby, he opens his Bible and reads the reassuring words of Psalm 121: "I will lift up my eyes to the hills. From where will my help come? My help comes from the Lord, who made Heaven and Earth."

… When the 10-minute service is over, Manly wipes his eyes. "I still get a little emotional after all these years, but I think I would be worried if I ever stopped." … He credits the county for honoring the dead, but says a common grave "just doesn't seem right."

The minister was right. We had to come back for Bill and Helen.

Honor thy Father and thy Mother

In November 2001, we returned to California and drove up to LA. I had called Craig the day before, and arranged for him to meet us. As we approached the cemetery, we were expecting to find something out of a Charles Dickens novel – dreary, unkempt, and forbidding. When we got there, we found exactly the opposite, starting with Craig's welcome. He was standing by the parking lot, waiting for us. A gentle, thoughtful man who has been the caretaker since 1984, he said that he liked the peace and quiet of the cemetery; it provided a refuge from the din and clamor of the city.

He led us into the chapel and showed us the ledger book containing the data about my father and explained the system – the date and place of death, the physician who reported it, the date of interment and the approximate burial location – Block B1, Row 3, Gravesites 9 and 10. The ledger listed a few claims by family members,

Potter's Field, Los Angeles County Cemetery

but there were many, many more whose ashes were unclaimed –
including my father's. Thinking about that, I said that the ledger must
contain a great deal of sadness; Craig responded simply that it
certainly had a lot of memories.

We went outside to a plot of ground just across the drive from the
chapel and crematory. It was the cemetery's Potter's Field, a name
descended from Biblical times denoting where the unclaimed,
indigent, and forgotten were buried. The attractive and well-tended
grounds, however, belied that grim heritage. There were mulberry and
apricot trees and rose beds. There were fat squirrels that came to filch
the peanuts that Craig kept in his shirt pocket. He was an easy mark
and they trusted him. Standing in the shade of the trees on a bright,
sunny day, I could not imagine a lovelier place for my father. There
was no sadness, just the memories.

There are no individual graves or stones in the mass burial
ground. The area is laid out in a large grid with round, numbered
cement discs indicating block and aisle numbers. These discs are
perhaps six inches in diameter and are set flat to the ground. Craig
apologized for the careless maintenance and mowing over the years
that had destroyed or covered many of the discs, including the one
that we sought. But we located B1/3 and by triangulating its location
with other discs we could zero in on the gravesite where Dad's ashes
and the ashes of all the others that died that year were buried.

I asked if I could have some of the soil to take back with us. It was
about as close to my father as we were going to get – a realization that

would unfold to families of the World Trade Center victims of 9/11. Craig got a shovel and started to dig for me, but then stopped and asked if I would prefer to do it. That gesture showed his unerring instinct for respect and dignity, and for offering comfort. We put the earth and a rose from the garden into a container, and thanked Craig for his kindness to us.

I had yet another task – to fill a container with some of the Pacific Ocean where my mother's ashes had been scattered after her death and cremation. She had reached the sea, "dead, shattered in all her parts," but once part of a larger life force. There was no specific site for her like there had been for my father. We simply found a quiet beach and filled a jar. Now we could go home.

The day before going to the cemetery in LA, we had stopped along the coast to see my cousin Alyce Ann – the Older Woman on whom I had a crush fifty-plus years earlier and had not seen since. She had developed a love for haiku and showed me her work. I admired many of her verses. Standing at the grave and then at the seashore where I symbolically reclaimed my father and mother, I tried to summarize the previous two years of research and discovery in 17 syllables, as Alyce might have:

> *We come from the hills.*
> *Our forebears return, transformed*
> *And show us ourselves.*

Earth and Water were two of the four elements that the ancient Greeks believed to have comprised the universe. My father and mother in the form of these elements were brought to Hanging Rock, Ohio. There, I dug once more in the shale, the thick clay, and the tangled roots that lay just beneath the grass on a steep slope in the cemetery. The family plot was getting a little crowded but there was room for one more gravestone. Sixty-four years after my father had died and eighteen years after my mother's death, Sue and I buried them under their own stone, next to my great-grandfather, my uncle, and my grandmother – the indomitable Maude Smith whom I had buried 35 years earlier. Then, from the Methodist Service of Death and Resurrection, I read:

God forever, your love is stronger than death. For the hope in you that faith gives, and for all your people who have laid hope on that faith, we praise you. Especially we lift up our hearts in thankfulness for the lives of Bill and Helen Moore whom you have taken to yourself so long ago.

We thank you for all that they meant to those who loved them and for everything in their lives that reflected your grace. We thank you that all suffering is past, and that, united with those they loved who have gone before us, they have entered into your joy. Let sorrow have its way with us, but let it not overwhelm us nor turn us against you. Work in us your will. Set our hands again to our tasks. And bring us at last to your home where we long to be.

In that prayer, I found myself keeping a promise that I had not realized I had made. For, under that stone, set in the foothills, only a river's width from Route 23, my parents lay together at last, surrounded by those who remembered and loved them, and united by the passionate love that Bill had expressed to Helen in his diary at Olive View so long ago. It was that diary and my father's words that had lived on, waiting for fulfillment. As their son, it was for me to remove the barriers that had kept them from their family and from one another. Now, those barriers were gone and they were "back home"— next to the iron and the river that flows below.

VI

Epilog

The tale had not quite ended. Sue and I had fitted together more pieces of the puzzle than we ever imagined when we began this odyssey. We had followed my ancestors from the Atlantic over the mountains and down river valleys to the Pacific to discover a legacy of struggle – of premature death for Bill and of what appears at this writing to be a tragic and lingering end for Helen. There were, however, pieces still missing, particularly those 30-plus years of my mother.

When Sue and I returned to LA in 2001 to claim my parents' ashes, we also tried to trace Harold whom Helen had listed on her pre-need certificate as "a friend". We learned that he had died in February 1999, aged 90; we had missed him by only 20 months. We did locate his brother Sidney who said that Harold had lived in an apartment on Figueroa, only five blocks from Helen. It was entirely possible that she moved into his apartment building and met him there, but Sidney had never heard mention of her. Now that I had Harold's last known address, I was able to locate several of Harold's neighbors who had lived at the apartment building at the time and asked them about Helen. One seemed to remember a "lively, chunky lady who traveled around town a lot on the bus," but did not know if it were she. The missing years were still that – missing.

"Shirt-tail" step-sisters
Sue and I had made three good friends in California – Selma, Bob, and Vivian – and, through Vivian, I discovered not one former stepsister but two – Phyllis and Shirley, who had been born to Bryant and his first wife Nellie. I wrote them when we returned to Bowling Green. Phyllis (nicknamed "Flip") immediately called me. She lived only three hours' driving time from us and there was no awkwardness or hesitation; she was warm, funny, and direct. We became friends immediately and a new chapter in the family history began to take shape.

Flip had a few surprises for me. She and her sister had been raised in Bowling Green! Flip also graduated from the University where I had taught for 35 years and had studied under several teachers who were now colleagues of mine. Their parents were married in Bowling Green and they had lived less than a mile from our home. They owned a bakery in town until it burned down in 1933. Nellie was buried in Bowling Green, next to her second husband, and there were two cousins still living in town. When she told me that she had also done her student teaching in Bowling Green, it struck me that yet another part of this history had come full circle. This town had been part and parcel of both our lives yet we did not realize it until over a half-century later. So near and yet so far.

Flip confirmed and expanded on Vivian's account of Bryant. She began by saying wistfully that "he could have become so much; he was bright and interesting." Instead, his struggles against childhood poverty and the Depression made him want to live the good life, make plenty of money, impress people, and be a "big shot." As a young man he desperately wanted to own a pair of white shoes but could not afford them. So he painted a pair and wore those. Bryant was also a philanderer and was unfaithful to Nellie. They separated in 1939; their divorce left Nellie embittered and deeply resentful of both my mother and Vivian. She never forgave any of the three and forbade any mention of their names ever in her presence. Phyllis' children met their grandfather only once or twice before he died. It was the same dynamics of estrangement and silence that had characterized Bill Moore's parents and infected that family.

According to Flip, Bryant and Helen moved to California in 1943 believing that a cousin, the race car driver Barney Oldfield, might help him find a job. She also said that the Navy was "after him for something that he had done." She could not remember the details, but implied that it was in her father's interest to become scarce in the Midwest.

Shirley was equally warm when I called her, but she, too, knew little of Helen. She described my mother as "blond and chunky" when they met in Toledo. Helen and Bryant lived in Detroit together before getting married. All three of them worked at the same plant but Helen was "upstairs in the office and I was in the plant". Bryant once again showed his ability to compartmentalize his life: "Daddy never mentioned that Helen had a son."

Shirley's recollection of her father paralleled Flip's – a pathetic man who tried to be something that he wasn't. She, like her sister, used the term "big shot." She also spoke of her mother's hatred toward Bryant and Helen, making them a topic never to be discussed: "If either of us even mentioned them, our mother wouldn't speak to us for a week." Shirley told the story of her own son's wedding when he created a crisis by wanting to invite both Nellie and Vivian. Shirley managed somehow to keep each unaware of the other's presence even during the wedding dinner where they sat practically back-to-back at separate tables.

Vivian, Phyllis, and Shirley told stories that were all too familiar. There had been so many instances in my father and grandmother's families where people nurtured old grudges and hatreds. They would not speak to one another of important things and tried to ignore the memories that went with them. They chose to ignore reality, even if it cost them something of their own wholeness and human-ness as well as that of their children and grandchildren. Perhaps it was from that urge to break down some walls that I had made copies of Bryant's letters to me to give to my new kin, showing them a side of their husband and father that they had not known. "Goodness knows he never wrote to me!" Vivian laughed. I pointed out to her that the letters were long and considerate, perhaps trying to make amends for the time and distance that had separated us. They were letters from someone who cared. "Yes," Vivian said; "he could be a very caring man." Flip, however, offered a caveat: "He could be a real pal, a daddy; but he never could be a father."

When she said that, I knew why my mother and he never took me back to California. My grandmother had witnessed first hand the destructiveness of alcohol on her own marriage and family, and had developed a hatred of it that was rabid. She *knew* what was happening to Helen and Bryant; it was no place in which to raise a child – *her* grandson. Bryant and Helen knew that same truth and would not have dared challenge her claim to me. Even though she could be vicious and scathing in her denunciation of behavior that she disliked, Maude never, in my presence said a word against my mother, my father, or my step-father.

Shirley then said to me: "You know, I never had a brother before!" "And I never had a sister," I replied. And when Sue and I finally met Flip, we immediately hugged like the "shirt-tail" step-sister and step-brother we had chosen to become. We would have no more with dysfunctional relationships, of thoughts unspoken, or of pretense.

The Present Generation

Although this story is primarily about my family roots, it would be short-sighted – and impolitic – to ignore the other end of the tree. Sue's support, insights, and hunches in this project have been invaluable; and it is only fair to give her and our children at least a few paragraphs.

Our marriage, like this project, has been full of surprises. I had known her in Portsmouth in the 1950's, where her father was a minister and her mother Mildred was a teacher. We met again at Case Western Reserve and began dating – for a while. The Moore's tendency to disappear, however, re-emerged when, abruptly, completely, and inexplicably, I stopped seeing Sue for nearly a year, even though we lived across Euclid Avenue from one another. A home-made Christmas card from her and a phone call of thanks from me, however, brought us back together and broke the family habit. Why did I stay away? I had no answer – which is what Grandfather Booker might have said to Stella if she had ever confronted him. Or perhaps he could have explained it to me.

Sue's father married us in 1962, and three years later Sarah was born in Hillsdale, Michigan, where I was teaching at the college. What to say about Hillsdale? It was an interesting two years, culminating in my contract not being renewed because of "my economic philosophy, which was contrary to the College's – which was free enterprise." That strained syntax belonged to the college president, whose autobiographical address to the faculty in 1964 was entitled: "Why Mediocre Men Succeed."

My "release" occasioned a couple of marches and picket signs, plus some articles in the Toledo *Blade* that were buried deep inside the local news. The mini-uproar, however, did enhance my modest reputation as something of a war hero when I went to Bowling Green State University. It was, after all, The Schizoid Sixties and rebellion was *de rigueur*.[45]

---

[45] Lewis Turco, "The Hillsdale Epistles," *Carleton Miscellany* VII:3 (Summer 1968), 17-32.

Hillsdale again made the papers in October 1999. This time, it was front-page stuff, full of Sex, Lies, (but no Videotape). There was, however, a Smoking Gun – literally. It seems that the wife of a history instructor claimed to have carried on a clandestine love affair with her father-in-law, who happened to be the president of the college. She felt betrayed when he divorced his wife only to marry someone else. After confronting Big Daddy with his perfidy, then confessing all to her cuckolded husband and the president's new wife, the jilted lover went to the college arboretum, put a .357 Magnum to her head, and pulled the trigger. It was a mess all around.[46]

The Conservative Right – that fearless bastion of free enterprise, rugged individualism, Pure Republicanism, and (above all) moral rectitude and High Family Values, was shocked – *shocked* – at what was going on at their darling college. After all, William Bennett and Bill Buckley had all but adopted the place, and Hillsdale had made a positive virtue of refusing any form of federal aid. *They* were not going to be dragged into the pit of sin, socialism, the Democratic Party, and the Welfare State. To them, the ACLU was a labor organization (!) that was to be avoided at all costs. Hillsdale would continue to teach only Those Truths That Made America Great.

But that was all before The Affair and The Suicide. From then on, it was as though someone had tried to meld *Who's Afraid of Virginia Woolf* with *The Stepford Wives Run Amok*. Although Bennett had resigned from the Board protesting the College's less-than-forthright handling of the case, William Buckley – a member of the presidential search committee – lobbied for none other than Ken Starr, nemesis of Bill Clinton and Monica Lewinsky, to become the new president. He would restore Hillsdale to the ranks of the mediocre. Buckley's effort fizzled, but its publicity could not have happened to a nicer school.

In 1965, we moved to Bowling Green, Ohio, with our new daughter. I taught American history and then became involved in arts education and administration until retiring 35 years later. Sue worked as a registered nurse, an alcoholism counselor, and as a social worker for the local hospice agency. While in Bowling Green, we added Amy, Andrew, and Wesley, along with a menagerie of dogs, cats, gerbils, fish, snakes, lizards and turtles (most of which met with

---

[46] Sam Tanenhaus, "Deadly Devotion," *Vanity Fair* (March 2000), 185-243.

disastrous fates). The children, however, survived their upbringing and got on with their lives:

Sarah married Benjamin Hirschl and had Elizabeth and Paul Michael while she was working on her doctorate in industrial and organizational psychology at Bowling Green and he was a salesman and credit manager. They moved to the West Coast in 1993 where Sarah began her university teaching and Ben worked for a credit union. They divorced in 1994; in 1998 she married Cooper Sherry, a junior high school choral conductor and organist for the church choir in which Sarah sang. Coop and Sarah had Olivia Yates in 1999.

Amy met Kate Meaker at Bowling Green State University while completing her second bachelor's degree. They became life companions, and moved to Penn State University, where Kate worked on her doctorate in statistics and Amy earned Master's degrees in music performance and in composition and history. They are living in the Washington, D. C., area where Kate is a government statistician and Amy is a secretary.

Andrew met Becky Barlow while both were studying for their master's degrees in public administration at Bowling Green. They eventually headed West and moved in with Sarah while seeking an apartment (and jobs). Becky went to work for an executive placement firm and Andrew located at a non-profit social service agency that trains and places workers who have disabilities. They then moved to Maryland in 1997 to be closer to Becky's parents (and us) and stayed with Amy and Kate while finding a home. Becky began working for another headhunting firm in Virginia, while Andrew became an independent home remodeler. Since then, he has become a computer programmer.

Wes nearly did not make it out of his infancy, thanks to two jealous cats that were caught in the nick of time as they were in his crib chewing on his three-day-old head. He survived, and eventually went to work for an engineering design company, but decided to follow his heart to become a drummer in a new age rock band. He had started to drum when he was still in diapers and as he grew older, he would practice by the hour in the garage – even when the temperature was freezing. Consequently, he has become a percussionist of exceptional quality and is performing on the West Coast.

The Living Cycle

In his *How Green Was My Valley*, Richard Llewellyn has written:

> I saw behind me those who had gone and before me those who are to come.

> I looked back and saw my father and his father and all our fathers, and in front to see my son and his son, and the sons upon sons beyond.

> And their eyes were my eyes.

> As I felt, so they had felt, and were to feel, as then, so now, as tomorrow and forever. Then I was not afraid, for I was in a long line that had no beginning and no end.

> And the hand of his father grasped my father's hand and his hand was in mine, and my unborn son took my right hand and all, up and down the line that stretched from Time That Was, to Time That Is and Is Not Yet, we all raised their hands to show the link.

> And we found that we were one, born of Woman, Son of Man, made in the Image, fashioned in the womb by the Will of God, the Eternal Father.

Family history is the interplay of time, emotions, and remembrance. It is ongoing. It is the celebration of individuals, the way by which fathers and sons, mothers and daughters, and lovers across the years once again link hands, tell stories, laugh, fight, and weep as though it were yesterday. Long-forgotten relatives – even the ones we did not much care for – come alive; old stories are re-told; neighborhoods on Second Street reappear like *Brigadoon*; and we realize just where our immortality lies – in the family and the memories it has created and preserved. Those memories tell us who we are and what we value.

Mike, Sue, Wesley, Andrew, Sarah, and Amy, 2000

My memory is redolent of Maude Smith who took me in and raised me as her own – to become a deep-dyed Presbyterian and Democrat, a son of Wooster who learned to love books and good writing, history and music; and one who valued loyalty and family above all else. In me, she placed her hope for the future. It was, however, a future that needed a past. I am now finding that past.

This family produced no famous or prominent people (well, not yet) but we raise our linked hands with as much pride as anyone. This might be one of the most precious gifts parents can give their children; and I invite our children, and their children, and their loved ones, and those who come after them, to add their chapters to a story that will be preserved and cherished.

The grandchildren: Paul, Elizabeth, and Olivia

Michael Moore

About the Author:

Raised along the Ohio River in the foothills of the Appalachians, Michael Moore graduated from the College of Wooster and earned his Ph. D. at Case Western Reserve University, where he also sang in the Cleveland Orchestra Chorus under Robert Shaw. He joined the history faculty at Bowling Green State University, but later retrained in administration and arts education. He was an assistant dean, lobbyist to the state legislature, and finally the founder and director of an aesthetic education program that is currently affiliated with the educational division of Lincoln Center for the Performing Arts, New York.

Since retiring, he has been a trustee of Otterbein Homes and chair of one of its subsidiary retirement communities.

Printed in the United States
1028000004B/364